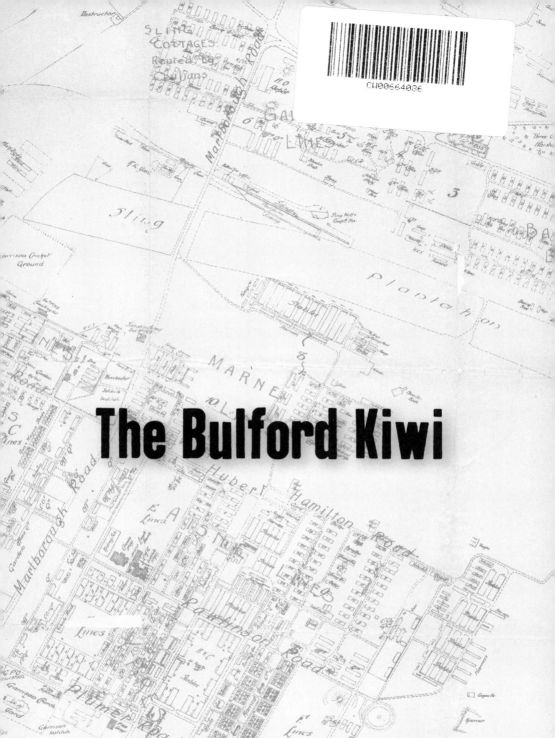

The Bulford Kiwi

The Bulford Kiwi

The kiwi We Left Behind

COLLEEN BROWN

Bateman

The author would like to acknowledge the support from the Kippenberger Literary Trust and the Chinese Poll Tax Heritage Trust in the preparation of this book.

Chinese Poll Tax Heritage Trust
華人人頭稅歷史遺產信託委員會

Book design: Nick Turzynski, redinc. Book Design, www.redinc.co.nz
Printed in China by Everbest Printing Company

Dedicated to Herbert (Bertie) Jarrett
1894–1919

*Bertie Jarrett (Service Number: 4/1944) with his
parents Ellen and George Jarrett, 1916.*

TANGI*
"Ko te tui e tangi atu i tou kainga
Te kowhai ki Aotearoa e karanga atu nei
Tui, tui, tui, tuitui-a ka rongo Te Po
Ka rongo Te Ao! Mauri ora e!
Moe mai takoto!"

Song of the tui in its chapel, the kowhai of Aotearoa
A lament, a celebration, searching, seeking
Searching at the altars of peace for the serenity of life
The Long Night, the Cold Night, now 'tis Light. Ah, 'tis Life!
Rest in Peace

DR HAARE WILLIAMS, PAPAKURA, JUNE 2017

*Tangi — to mourn, cry, but also to sing and celebrate

Contents

Foreword

SOME OF THE MOST REWARDING THINGS WE DO IN LIFE ARE NOT PREMEDITATED OR THOUGHT THROUGH; THEY JUST HAPPEN, DRIVEN BY EVENTS, COINCIDENCES AND GOODWILL.

One such event was the restoration of the Bulford Kiwi, completed by the best soldiers I have ever known; the Arctic Warriors of 249 Signal Squadron (Ace Mobile Force Europe) in 1980.

The Warriors were motivated by beer, extra days off, and a chance to restore an overgrown chalk monument while waiting to go abroad.

At that time we didn't know anything of the politics surrounding the Kiwi. We just sorted it out and went off to do our exercise in Turkey.

On our return the story of the Kiwi began to unfold, and the Warriors took a great pride in being able to have done something to honour our brothers in arms from New Zealand who gave so much and endured horrendous hardship in the defence of the mother country thousands of miles away from their homeland.

We adopted the kiwi as our symbol of unity, and began the annual Kiwi Trophy march and shoot competition. This wasn't planned to be an enduring event. It was just a bit of military fun to keep us fit and motivated while we awaited the Soviet onslaught. We never dreamt it would still be flourishing thirty-six years later.

The story could have ended there, with tales of the good old days seen from the bottom of a beer glass at reunions. This was not to be. From the land of the Long White Cloud came Colleen Brown, a most determined lady (and now an honorary Arctic Warrior) who has pieced together the

New Zealand Chief of Staff Major General Brian Poananga, left, presenting Danny Fisher with a commemorative shield for his work on the Bulford Kiwi, 1981.

story of the Kiwi for all to read. This is a story of valour, tragedy, human endeavour, hope and reconciliation.

We who have had a small part to play in this story thank her for all she has done and hope this enthuses others not to forget those brave soldiers of the Great War, but to honour them with an everlasting memorial.

LIEUTENANT COLONEL DANNY FISHER MBE, DL

Introduction

ALL STORIES HAVE A STARTING POINT. THIS BOOK STARTED WITH A SEPIA PHOTO AND SOME UNANSWERED QUESTIONS. I WAS GIVEN A PHOTOGRAPH OF MY GREAT UNCLE BERTIE JARRETT SEATED BESIDE HIS ADOPTIVE PARENTS, MY GREAT GRANDPARENTS, BEFORE HE WENT OFF TO WAR IN 1916. AS IN SO MANY NEW ZEALAND FAMILIES, THE PHOTO HAD BEEN PASSED DOWN THE GENERATIONS, THE BLUE PENCIL WRITING ON THE BACK BARELY LEGIBLE ANY MORE. WITH THE PHOTO CAME BERTIE'S STORY.

The photo was carried by Bertie throughout the war; through the hell of France and right back to Sling Camp on Salisbury Plain in Southern England where he was sent after the Armistice in 1918. Bertie Jarrett died in Tidworth Military Hospital of pneumonia, early in March 1919, while waiting for a ship to take him home. Bertie's belongings returned to New Zealand, but he didn't. Bertie lies in the Tidworth Military Cemetery near the site of Sling Camp. He left behind in New Zealand a fiancée who never married, my devastated great grandparents, and his extended family. To survive the nightmare of the Western Front only to die of pneumonia seemed the cruellest of fates. Another tragic irony in Bertie's life was that at five feet one-and-a-half inches (156.2 cm) he was under the regulation height for enlisted men. He may have been excused war service on that basis, but he volunteered anyway.

Bertie's photo has hung on our lounge wall as part of a family collection for years. The question that I could never really fathom was why did Bertie, who enlisted early in the war, have to wait nearly four months for a boat home? I decided to look into it. Every time I researched his war grave and the surrounding military area of Salisbury Plain, and the New Zealand Expeditionary Force's occupation of Sling Camp, an image of and information about the giant Kiwi carved into Beacon Hill in 1919 kept popping up in front of me.

And so the journey began.

The more I dug into the story about this huge excavation on the side of a prominent hill overlooking Sling Camp, the more fascinated I became. It was like a puzzle set in front of me to decipher. There was no roadmap, and the highways and byways I've taken since have been, at times, impulsive with rich rewards and, at other times, barren after a great deal of time and effort. But bit by bit the story has emerged.

This is a book of questions. The questions that were rarely asked of our returning soldiers from WWI until those experiences were sixty years and more distant in their memories. Questions about why it took so long for our soldiers to return from the battlefields of Europe and beyond to this most remote of part of the British Empire. Questions about what they did and felt at the end of the war and what it all meant to them.

It is about why we, modern New Zealanders, know little about the history that surrounds this important time at the end of this war and our soldiers' repatriation.

The aim of this story is to put the spotlight on events that happened nearly a century ago. I am not a military historian, nor do I pretend to be one. The book is more of a social history of a time we know little about. Throughout the book I have used the voices of those soldiers who wrote so eloquently about that time. It is their story. It is our story as a nation. It is an understatement to say that I was moved by those scribbled notes and recordings. There is something unbearably affecting about sitting in the National Library in Wellington holding a diary written nearly a hundred years ago by a soldier who had been through the most unimaginable horrors for years, with only brief respite through leave, sickness or injury. The words and photos of those men accompanied me as I described their wartime experiences. I became so familiar with their stories that it was as though they egged me on to include this part, and not to dare leave that part out either. For me the book is unapologetically emotional. I was moved, and similarly I want to move you, the reader.

This book also tells about the families left behind and the stories they handed down over the generations and their place in the hearts of those families, about their lives, their war experiences and their grief. There is no doubt in my mind that our returning soldiers grieved for their lost youth, for the fruitlessness of war, for the death of their wartime friends and the wiping out of all those mates they had grown up with.

When reading the diaries and letters that remain, the anguish of those young men is almost palpable. They came home, saying very little of their experiences, and got on with their lives in the best way they knew how. And their families have held on to these treasures, labelling them as 'letters from the front' or 'my uncle's last letter home'. Those men's lives are our lives too. They have shaped who we are as a people, as a country.

The Bulford Kiwi is an intriguing story that draws you in. Its genesis comes from the tedium of post-war military routines and exercises along with well-meaning but often poorly received compulsory education classes. The men at the centre of this story, along with their commanding officers, were for the most part citizen soldiers who had 'done their bit' for the country and now just wanted to go home. The Kiwi emblem was born out of a riot and completed on the day that peace was eventually signed in June 1919.

References about this time in our history are usually sparse, devoting at best a paragraph or two to the Bulford Kiwi and the March 1919 riot. But by asking more questions and digging through old documents, I found family members across the country who opened up their old file boxes, dusted off photographs, and read back through old letters, generously contributing them to the mix.

These people's generosity in sharing their stories has left me speechless at times. Early on in the journey and following a lead I called two phone numbers in Whanganui. On the second call I struck gold in the purest form. Did the family have a diary of their WWI family member? Yes, they had a transcript of Great Uncle Harry's diary. Did I want it? Absolutely! Give me your email, they said, and we'll send it to you tonight. Really! I was also instructed to talk to Aunty Margaret, the matriarch of the family who knew everything. And at the bottom of Aunty Margaret's huge plastic box containing that same Uncle Harry's WWI memorabilia, we found a small brown envelope. On the outside of the envelope in pencil was written the words 'Sling Camp'. Inside that envelope were a number of negatives of the Bulford Kiwi. They had been sitting there for nearly a hundred years. They are now part of the book and this story.

From those eclectic contributions, and there have been many, has emerged information about a group of men whose deeds have remained little known until now. Men whose diaries have been uncovered, whose letters home have been unearthed and whose photographs of that time have all become part of this narrative.

Bit by bit the Kiwi has revealed its past. Who would have thought that the giant Kiwi was drawn by a soldier who after the war would become a successful Auckland businessman? Who knew that the New Zealand soldier who surveyed the Kiwi onto the slopes of Beacon Hill was from the first Chinese family in New Zealand? Who knew that the captain, who chivvied the fatigue parties up the hill six days a week, attested to serve his country twice in WWI and was a survivor of a horrendous explosion in the trenches that buried him alive, had written a diary describing his experiences?

Whether they knew it or not at the time, over the years the construction of the Kiwi emblem became a touchstone for returning servicemen and their families. A chore to occupy the hours of waiting for a ship home had become something to be proud of; the detested Sling Camp was now adorned with a connection to home. The emblem came to represent far more than a mere motif. For many of those involved in creating it, the Kiwi came to represent the lost men, the men whose feet had trod the training bullring where they readied themselves for war, and those who would never go home. A monument built by soldiers, not governments, for themselves and their mates.

But the story does not end with the construction of the Kiwi or with the closing of the gate to Sling Camp for the last time in November 1919, leaving the maintenance of the Kiwi in the hands of the Kiwi Polish Company.

The book is in two parts. The first part deals with the end of the war, the factors that delayed the men returning to New Zealand, the two-day riot and its aftermath, and describes the actual construction of the 1919 Kiwi. The second part of the book continues the story of what happened to the Kiwi after the soldiers left for home and peacetime routines were established in England.

The bond between soldier and place is described by George Jenkins when he returns to the site where Sling Camp stood and he sets eyes on the Kiwi fifteen years after leaving for home. The connection to the Kiwi is also told in Percy Blenkarne's advocacy to the New Zealand Government in the 1950s for them to 'pick up' the cost of maintaining the emblem, a part of New Zealand remaining in England forever.

And for a while the New Zealand Government did honour their pledge to those soldiers from WWI. They did pay for some maintenance work to be done, but not enough. Essentially, we as a country forgot about the Kiwi. We gracelessly let it go. We were careless of an emblem entrusted to us as a country by those soldiers. Then in 1980, after many of those soldiers had died, when asked to save the Kiwi from extinction by an officer on behalf of the British Army the New Zealand Government declined to help. In doing so, it formally relinquished any ownership of the giant bird.

At this point the story may well have come to a sad conclusion. However, like all good yarns there was a hero waiting in the wings to do the deed that needed to be done. Fittingly it was a British soldier from another generation who saw what was required, gathered his men around him and restored the Kiwi.

This is a book about a gift from our soldiers that was ours as a nation to keep and honour. And as a country we thoughtlessly let it slip away from us. Nevertheless it is our story and it should be told.

COLLEEN BROWN, AUGUST 2017

Part One

The Bulford Kiwi

CARVED INTO THE SLOPES OF BEACON HILL IN SOUTHERN ENGLAND IS THE CHALKY-WHITE FIGURE OF A KIWI. IT LOOKS ACROSS THE SALISBURY PLAIN TOWARDS THE ENGLISH PORTS WHERE NEW ZEALAND SOLDIERS DISEMBARKED DURING WWI.

In 1919, the remnants of that same New Zealand Army cut the kiwi emblem by hand into the green pastures above their base at Sling Camp before they sailed back to New Zealand. They left a lasting memento of their stay in Europe and their participation in the many theatres of war.

Sling Camp, where thousands of New Zealand soldiers trained before encountering the horrors of trench warfare, no longer exists. But the Kiwi remains.

'The camp they occupied has gone, but the foundations of their huts can still be seen in the Crescent when the grass is low and the shadows fall aright.'[1]

This is the story of why and how the Bulford Kiwi was constructed. It is about ordinary men in the citizen army of New Zealand who survived a devastating conflict.

And at the end of that war those soldiers just wanted to go home.

– Chapter One –

Home Shores on the Horizon: November 1918

Hurrah for our side! can you realise hostilities have ceased? . . . here there is no excitement, no celebrations; everything is going on in the same old way. not even a cheer was raised when first we heard the official news. but away deep down there is the knowledge that soon we shall be seeing the home shores appearing on the horizon and that is what the signing of the armistice means to us, it means home and loved ones once more, the sooner the quicker eh? [1]

BERT STOKES, NOVEMBER 1918

These words came from Bombardier Bertram (Bert) Stokes in a letter written to his parents while he was in France and dated 18 November 1918. However it would be another seven months before Bert Stokes saw home shores and his loved ones again.[2]

Why did it take so long to get soldiers like Bert Stokes back to their 'home shores'?

The end of the Great War in 1918 was rapid. Once Armistice had been declared on 11 November 1918, the plans to demobilise New Zealand soldiers were put into effect. Sling Camp on Salisbury Plain in Southern England had been selected to be the collection and demobilisation point for the over 40,000 New Zealand troops stationed across Europe and Britain.

It should not be underestimated just how much the New Zealand soldiers longed to be back in New Zealand. The connection to home was the most constant of companions throughout the war. There are many letters and postcards found in libraries, and archives, along with those carefully kept by families over the generations, from soldiers asking about home.

George Jenkins' family kept many of the letters he sent home relating his wartime experiences from the time of his departure from New Zealand in July 1917 to his imminent return as a wounded soldier early in 1919. The uncensored parts of George's letters refer to the family farm in Whakapirau in Northland and his concern as to how his father was managing to keep it going on his own.

George viewed the countryside around him in England and France with a farmer's eye, assessing the crops and the health of the stock, and making observations about the different farming methods used. His writing reveals several things that bridged the gap between home and the foreignness of England: certain records played on the phonograph; the eagerly awaited food parcels, especially if they contained butter; magazines and newspapers; and knitted garments. From time to time George passed on suggestions to his father about the farm and clearly stated that he should sell it if the worst came to the worst and he couldn't manage any more. While the letters are pragmatic and thoughtful, with an affectionate sign off at the end, there is a thread of wonder in his letters at how a young man like himself had travelled so far for this war.[3]

Often letters and the framed sepia photograph of their 'boy' in his pristine khaki army uniform were all families had left of the young man who set out on his huge adventure to the other side of the world — letters like the one Private Lloyd wrote to his parents in Taranaki in February 1918 asking about the farm and the productivity of particularly the cows and bees. He writes, 'I think of you all in distant New Zealand very often, but it doesn't pay, I get pretty homesick. I hope to see you all again when the war is over.'[4]

But unlike Bert Stokes and George Jenkins, Private Lloyd never saw his family or the farm at Manaia again. He died of bullet wounds, a prisoner of war in September 1918, aged twenty-one.

Sixty-eight years after Bert Stokes wrote his letter to his parents celebrating the end of the war, he was interviewed about his war experiences. He wistfully reflected that when the New Zealand soldiers did get leave from the trenches during the war, they travelled from France with British troops who crowded to the front of the boat eager to see the white cliffs of Dover and knowing that once the boat docked they would see their wives, mothers, sweethearts and families. 'We had nothing like that,' Bert says. 'We were just going on holiday.'[5] And after that the New Zealanders just returned to the trenches.

So naturally the New Zealand soldiers looked towards home. Many, like Bert Stokes, had spent years away and yearned for home, as in Bert's words to his folks in New Zealand, 'the sooner the quicker'.[6]

While the New Zealand soldiers at the Western Front may not have outwardly celebrated the Armistice announcement, there was profound relief felt throughout New Zealand. The celebrations, although impromptu and heartfelt, were somewhat muted because of the influenza pandemic affecting the nation. Plans for formal celebrations came later. Everyone looked forward to the prospect of the troops coming home. However, it soon became clear that transporting thousands of soldiers back to New Zealand wasn't going to be plain sailing.

Brigadier-General George Richardson, an experienced soldier based in London who had invaluable administrative skills, was in charge of making sure that the demobilisation and repatriation process to New Zealand proceeded in an orderly fashion. The planning for repatriation had started in New Zealand in 1914 and was consolidated in London during the latter part of 1918. But that carefully considered planning was no match for the sheer volume of men needing to be repatriated and the unexpected social upheaval that occurred in Britain after Armistice was declared.

There was no blueprint for this type of exercise. Richardson had already discovered shipping unfit men to New Zealand was problematic even before the Armistice was declared. When challenged by a New Zealand newspaper about the number of unfit men remaining in Britain, Richardson provided the answers in a letter to Sir James Allen, the Minister of Defence, on 6 December 1918, stating that the assertion was true 'but I have not been able to get the ships to take them back to the Dominion.'[7] Added to the turmoil surrounding the end of the conflict was the fact that ships to transport the soldiers were at a premium, and New Zealand was not the only country looking to repatriate its men.

The logistics of organising the demobilisation of thousands of troops and then repatriating them to New Zealand was further complicated by the fact that the New Zealand force in Europe was split between France and Britain.

Many New Zealand soldiers already stationed in France when Armistice was declared were needed as part of the British occupying force in Germany. Major General Sir Andrew Russell, who commanded the New Zealand Division on the Western Front, understood the immediate post-war situation only too well. From a military perspective, Britain and its Allies had to secure a peace agreement as soon as possible after the Armistice was declared. One way of making sure the ceasefire was not broken was to occupy important parts of Germany. However, from a humanitarian point of view, Russell acknowledged that New Zealand troops needed to return home as speedily as could be arranged. So there lay the tension between helping to obtain peace and completing the commitment made to Britain at the start of the conflict versus getting the men home.

The key objective as part of an international military force was to secure peace, therefore, late in 1918 New Zealand soldiers, as part of the occupation force, marched from France through to the Rhine in Germany, a trek of some 240 kilometres. The wintery conditions were harsh. Food supplies could not keep pace with the advance into Germany and were insufficient to meet the needs of the belly of an army on the march.

Records of that journey differ in emphasis and content between published 'official' accounts and a diary written by an ordinary soldier.

Colonel Hugh Stewart, a respected academic from Canterbury College Christchurch, a decorated and experienced soldier, had commanded the Second Battalion Canterbury Regiment during the war. In 1920, back in New Zealand, Stewart wrote the official history of the New Zealand Division from researching and analysing extensive official war diaries, orders, reports and personal accounts available to him.

Stewart's description of that episode emphasises the warmth of the welcomes the men received from liberated villagers as they marched. He comments on the scenery and the historical attributes of some villages, making the march 'interesting and enjoyable'.[8] Stewart does briefly mention that despite the High Command stating that the comfort of the troops should be a top priority, on the march into Germany the roads were poor, the weather 'vile' and the men suffered from worn out boots and a lack of supplies.

Captain David Ferguson, documenting the history of the Canterbury Regiment, concurs with Stewart's account, stating that the men suffered 'a good deal of discomfort' from poor footwear not designed for long marches and acknowledging that the rations given to the men were 'insufficient' for the march into Germany.[10]

None of the authorised accounts recorded what was done to improve the soldiers' conditions. The emphasis is on the glory of marching into Germany and the responses from the liberated towns along the way.

Lieutenant Arthur Byrne, writing the official Otago regimental record after the war, notes that there were some soldiers who felt that the army should be preparing to get its troops back to New Zealand rather than being part of the occupying force in Germany. Byrne discounted those opinions as coming from newly arrived soldiers in France. Byrne echoes the common view that it was an honour for New Zealand to be selected to march into Germany. He does acknowledge that rain fell for a number of days during the march, but reports that the men were provided with comfortable billets, hot baths and fresh changes in underwear, along with warm welcomes from the liberated civilians.[11]

The deprivations endured by ordinary soldiers were more colourfully described in John O'Connell's diary. Private O'Connell, aged 20, was in the First Auckland Battalion 32nd reinforcements. His total active service in the war was just on two years' duration. He was a foot soldier on that long march. He kept a detailed record of life en route to Germany, particularly referring to the basic necessities for a soldier: food, equipment, shelter and warmth. It makes bleak reading.

There was nothing 'interesting and enjoyable' on that march as recorded by O'Connell from 25 November 1918. In his rounded school-boy writing O'Connell's diary logs the scanty provisions for the men, the exhausting marches, the bitter weather, and the relentless activities of rats and fleas at night as soldiers tried to sleep.

The soldiers marched for hours on end in all weathers. Despite the troops remaining vigilant throughout the night, rats often ate their rations, and there were no replacements for the lost provisions. Soldiers became sick through lack of food, exhaustion, the weight of their packs and the cold wet weather. O'Connell does acknowledge the heartfelt welcome the troops received from locals as they entered each town on the march, however many of his entries focus on his daily preoccupations with food, feet and vermin.

O'Connell dispassionately documents the state of his feet as the advance into Germany progresses: 26 November 1918 — 'feet all bleeding through the cobbles'.[12] On 28 November 1918 O'Connell stated that his feet were bleeding and sore. The army doctor he saw gave him some lint and told him to carry on. On 30 November his feet were 'all blistered and stuck to my sox'.[13] That night there was no food left for his contingent when they arrived at their billet – a cowshed full of rats. O'Connell noted that he was too 'tired and hungry to worry'.[14]

O'Connell's diary entry for Friday 29 November is a typical matter-of-fact run sheet of events. He was up at 2.30 a.m. and some hours later had breakfast of four biscuits and a mug of tea during the march at 7.30 a.m. O'Connell states that after marching all day his billet was a French house without a roof and as it rained all night the troops woke up the following morning stiff with the cold and starving.

On 1 December 1918, he reflects on the march when the New Zealand troops entered Mauberge in Belgium: 'I managed to see it out carrying my boots on my shoulders but it was hard all the same.'[15] He spent part of that night trying to sleep under a tree in a park but had to shift due to a light fall of snow.

In early December some of the New Zealand troops had had enough. O'Connell notes that on 5 December, after 11 days of relentless marching, poor diet and overwhelming exhaustion the men of the Second Battalion refused to carry their packs any further. There is no mention in O'Connell's diary of what was done to resolve the men's grievances. However Brigadier-General Herbert Hart wrote in his war diary that on 7 December the troops 'discarded steel helmets, great coats and entrenching tools.'[16] For the remainder of the march the troops were only asked to carry a light pack with a change of underclothes, leather jerkins and a ground sheet. Two blankets per soldier were carried on trucks. So after the small insurrection on 5 December an order must have been issued allowing the men to carry a lighter load.

O'Connell records a red letter day when on 15 December he had his first bath in eight weeks. He changed his clothes as well but observed that the ones he had taken off were in the same state as the ones he was required to put on.

O'Connell's diary entries finish on 21 December 1918, when he reached Germany. It is worth noting the last entry in his diary, which recounts that final brutal march that started at 2.30 a.m. with a meal of two biscuits and a slice of bacon. The troops trudged in the sleet, crossing the Belgian border and entering Germany at 6.30 a.m. They marched through Germany for two hours, reaching a train station at nine o'clock, and waited for an hour in the cold with their packs on until the train arrived to take them to Cologne. At the station the soldiers were issued with a cake of chocolate and some biscuits to sustain them for the six-hour rail trip that followed. On reaching the outskirts of Cologne the men then marched across the Rhine and on until 1.30 a.m. on Sunday 22 December. O'Connell's concluding entry for the day reads, 'we were that tired that we fell in full marching order after being on the move since 3.30 Saturday morning and covering 80 odd miles'.[17]

John O'Connell would have found it hard to reconcile some of the official narratives of that episode in the New Zealand Army's history with his own recorded experiences.

Another ordinary soldier also details the hardship encountered on that march, but his version of events records in full the very stirring welcome the troops received from people in towns liberated by the Allies. Private Monty Ingram's diary gives deeper personal reflections on his feelings as he marched towards Germany. Monty Ingram was obviously moved by the reception the New Zealand troops received, painting a vivid picture of the thousands of cheering residents pressing in on the soldiers as they entered the town of Verviers near the Belgian-German border. The columns of marching soldiers had flowers showered over them, flags waved from windows and young women joined the soldiers as they marched.

At the start of the march Monty was critical of the need for New Zealand soldiers to be part of the army of occupation but at the end of it, once he has reached his destination he wrote, 'Now the march is over, I'm glad that I participated in it. The experience was well worthwhile. I shall not soon forget the thrill of marching behind playing bands through villages and towns where every house was made gay by the fluttering flags of the Allies, and where the whole populace lined the streets to cheer us in excited welcome.'[18]

By early 1919 the majority of the New Zealand troops sent to occupy Germany were on their way back to Britain. Most of them had left Cologne by the end of March 1919 to join the remaining New Zealand troops awaiting repatriation.

And so the mammoth task began to get New Zealand troops assembled in centralised embarkation hubs from where they had been stationed within Europe or Britain, organise appropriate shipping and manage the soldiers' return on a lengthy sea voyage.

A demobilisation document published before the end of the war stipulates that it was the New Zealand Government's wish to see the return of all New Zealand troops to the Dominion in the shortest possible time. The paper argues that as New Zealand had sent a larger percentage of its population to the war than any other country in the British Empire and had a great need for the men to return home to get the economy moving again, it recommends that six ships per month should be the absolute minimum allocation for New Zealand troops from Europe. The memorandum states quite clearly that its preference is for ships to travel from New Zealand laden with farm products for the British population weary of war rationing and return home with a cargo of soldiers and supplies for the industrial needs of the Dominion.[19]

Brigadier-General Richardson and the New Zealand Headquarters' staff were responsible for the camps where the troops were stationed. However, moving New Zealand troops into and out of theatres of war and back to New Zealand came under the direct authority of the British Imperial Army. Therefore, to a large extent, the New Zealanders relied on the good organization of the British to make sure the process proceeded according to the NZEF demobilisation schedule and without too many setbacks.

Brigadier-General Richardson knew his men and understood that they were restive and wanted to get home. He knew that if repatriation was delayed for any reason there would be trouble.

Richardson was proved right on all counts. The men were restive, there were delays and there was trouble.

‒ Chapter Two ‒

Demobilisation: November–December 1918

LONDON, 23 November 1918
Demobilisation cards are already being issued to the New Zealand forces.
The 1914 class will return first, and each succeeding class in rotation. Sling
Camp, on the Salisbury Plain, becomes the demobilisation centre.[1]
EVENING POST

The mission of demobilising the New Zealand Expeditionary Force (NZEF) officially started on 30 December 1918. It was a complex and unenviable task. With more than forty thousand troops scattered across Europe, some stationed in Germany as part of the occupying force, and with troops under the overall command of the British Imperial Army, it was an organisational nightmare.[2]

At the same time as Brigadier-General Richardson was trying to marshal the New Zealand troops according to the dictates of his demobilisation orders, the British Government was endeavouring to manage the millions of its troops returning home plus all the other Dominions' troops under its control. It was a time of intense social turmoil in Britain as the government grappled with the problem of how to manage and absorb its returning soldiers back into a dramatically changed society.

The basic intent of the New Zealand demobilisation plan was to return the troops in order of their length of service and not by the units in which they served. Soldiers were also to be sent back by broad geographical sections rather than by battalions. Sling Camp near Salisbury was to be the main demobilising hub.

Prior to the scheme for demobilisation being finalised, officers commanding various sections of the New Zealand regiments were asked to comment on the scheme.

Some prophetic comments in response to the demobilisation proposal came from Auckland Regiment's Lieutenant-Colonel McKenzie who had been a serving officer from 1916. On 21 November 1918 he states, 'I do not agree to the Division being sent back by Districts. I consider that if sent back by Battalions, as under existing organisations, much confusion would be saved and it would be easier to maintain discipline.' In addition he says, 'I do not agree to the proposition of bringing all branches of the Service to Sling Camp.'[3] Lieutenant-Colonel McKenzie states that with four ships sailing per month a whole battalion in each district could be sent home. Unfortunately McKenzie's comments were not heeded and the original plan was sanctioned.

Other comments from commanding officers warned about the risk of accommodation at Sling Camp getting over crowded if the movements of men between Europe to Sling Camp and from Sling to New Zealand were not synchronised.

Brigadier-General Robert Young mentions his disquiet about getting the men home in a letter written in November to his wife Belle. Young tells his wife not to expect him home any time soon. He adds that it wasn't for one to 'hand in one's ticket and ask to get out of it. There is a lot of work to be done and the future of New Zealand depends on the way the men are got back to their various occupations.'[4]

He then adds a word of caution similar to the words of other officers who had served in the field: ' If all the senior officers they know clear off home the end will develop into a rabble very probably.'[5]

On 25 November 1918 a booklet on demobilisation was issued by the Administrative Headquarters of the New Zealand Expeditionary Forces (NZEF) to all ranks.[6] It laid out the details for an orderly and managed release of troops, and their return to New Zealand. The booklet states that approximately 50,000 men needed to be repatriated from France and the United Kingdom, and another 3000 from Egypt. The document states that it was anticipated that repatriation would take about nine months from the time the demobilisation orders were issued.

On the surface it appeared to be a logical and well planned set of arrangements.

Troops deemed fit for active service and referred to as 'Group A' men were expected to remain in Britain until the British Imperial Army was confident that the November 1918 Armistice would last and a peace agreement would be signed. They were sent to Sling Camp to await transportation home. Soldiers deemed unfit for active service were returned to New Zealand during the Armistice period.

Shipping best suited to the needs of the troops was to be made available by the Ministry of Shipping controlled by the British Government.

The remaining troops were then grouped into classes. The first group of men to be homeward bound were referred to as the 1914 Class and included troops from the 1914 Main Body to the second reinforcements. The 1915 troops were classified as the 1915 Class and contained men from the third to the eighth reinforcement and so on through to the 1918 Class which ended with the 43rd reinforcements, the last soldiers to leave New Zealand for the war.

A number of strands and sub-sets lay within the basic instructions for a priority return to New Zealand. The troops were further split out depending upon whether they were married or needed in New Zealand for essential services or for reasons of domestic hardship. Soldiers' wives and families living in Great Britain would also be repatriated when appropriate ships were available.

It is obvious from the follow-up routine orders at Sling Camp that the men did not fully understand the decisions surrounding the order of repatriation. In a Group Routine Order 57 in early March 1919,[7] unit commanders were ordered to 'explain carefully' to their men the repatriation process which had been detailed in a 7 January 1919 order. Group Order 57 laid out the different classes of men and clearly confirmed that apprentices and those studying degrees were to get a ship home before those within the same class as them. Single men had to make way for married men. The need to reinforce the original orders issued to the waiting soldiers seems to indicate that senior staff were aware of the soldiers' lack of understanding, and also that the men were unhappy about the priorities awarded to their fellow soldiers.

The logistical combinations were challenging and would have tested the most efficient of administrators.

In essence, the units of men who had fought together often in the harshest conditions were sliced and diced in the demobilisation process and split apart. Some commanding officers were separated from their men, many of whom they had commanded through very difficult circumstances. As Lieutenant-Colonel McKenzie had predicted, taking away the established layer of command exposed and weakened the trusted officer-to-men communication lines, and the way in which orders were received and interpreted by the various ranks. Men who had served and survived the war together were separated. Frustrations grew.

All troops were to be shipped home to a port near their unit's base. This meant, for example, that all units from the upper North Island were to go to Auckland, the men from across the southern stretch of the South Island to Dunedin, and so forth.

All spheres of planning and organisation from the New Zealand administration section of the army relied on the efficiency of the British Government. In turn the Ministry of Shipping controlled shipping availability for all countries using British ports. The New Zealand Government had little to no say over shipping movements to New Zealand during the period of demobilisation and repatriation.

Psychologically New Zealand soldiers' hearts and minds were pointed towards home. They sniffed freedom and an end to army life, an opportunity to get on with their personal lives, to see their wives and children, their parents. For some there was now the possibility of marriage.

Yes, the soldiers had signed up to fight for King and country and yes, they had promised to obey all the orders handed down to them until they were discharged from army life. However, the Armistice was secured, and now in their minds their job was done. They were back to being essentially civilians wearing a uniform. They needed to go home.

As the winter months dragged on, so the feelings of resentment and disgruntlement grew. The tough march into Germany had not been universally popular with the men. Bonded units were broken up, and comrades left for home and freedom.

However, the major challenges to the repatriation plan came not from within the Ministry of Shipping controlled by the British Government, but unpredictably from disaffected British workers demanding better working conditions after the war. Prior to the war, there had been a great deal of industrial strife in Britain. The war years provided a temporary hiatus in industrial confrontations, but straight after Armistice was declared, workers across the country were determined to re-kindle their efforts for fairer working conditions, not only for those in work but also for the unemployed. Strike action centred on the state-owned railways, mines and docks. It was worker against the state. The strikers' actions in January and February 1919 had an immediate effect on New Zealand troops waiting to return home. The ships stopped moving, the docks were immobilised and the trains halted. The soldiers waiting to go home were caught; no transport, no repatriation.

To keep the men occupied until they were repatriated they had four hours a day, six days a week of compulsory education classes to help reintegrate them back into civilian life and the workforce.

Brigadier-General Richardson was a keen supporter of the ambitious education programme devised in 1917 initially to help reintegrate wounded soldiers back into the workforce, and to help fill their spare time. When the New Zealand Expeditionary Force was faced with the possibility of it taking up to eighteen months to demobilise their soldiers, the scheme was expanded to include the soldiers awaiting repatriation.

The aim of the education scheme was based on the principle that the country owed a debt to those who had fought in its civilian army, especially now that the hostilities had finished. The majority of the NZEF had been volunteers, some of whom had little work experience, and now they needed to be reabsorbed back into civilian life. The programme aimed to teach the troops about citizenship and help them gain employment once they reached home. Instructors were for the main part drawn from the army itself.

A comprehensive plan for what a full education programme would look like was worked through at a conference in London in April 1918. Once the Armistice was signed, the compulsory education scheme, covering a wide variety of subjects, was offered to all soldiers. The New Zealand government contributed £50,000 to the organisation. Over 13,000 men attended classes at Sling Camp.

While it was undoubtedly conceived with the very best of intentions, and was a great opportunity for the troops, for some, the compulsory classes smacked of being an extension of army life, the life they were trying so desperately to put behind them. The troops just wanted to go home.[8]

For many, being incarcerated in Sling Camp brought back bitter memories of training there as raw recruits. As long as it was merely a temporary stop-off point as part of the demobilisation process it could be tolerated.

But this was not to be.

~ Chapter Three ~

Sling Camp: January–February 1919

17 June 1917
This bleak unlovely prison, Sling, is the chief New Zealand training camp.
A man cannot call his soul his own.[1]
N M INGRAM NO 42110

Sling Camp. Virtually every New Zealand soldier had a view about this training ground located in the middle of the Salisbury Plain. Few were complimentary about it. They had trained there as newly arrived soldiers from New Zealand. Many a soldier had returned to it after recuperating from injury or illness, to become battle-fit and ready for combat again on the Western Front.

And in 1919 there they were again, back in Sling Camp, waiting to go home.

The initial decision to locate New Zealand soldiers in Sling Camp in 1914 was a very deliberate one. It had to be close to transport hubs, France and the New Zealand Army Headquarters, and at the same time a safe distance from the tempting lights of London.

Salisbury Plain consists of a vast sweep of military camps and training grounds, owned by the British Ministry of Defence since 1898. Sling Camp, as part of that network, abutted Bulford Camp run by the Imperial Army, separated only by Sling Plantation.

Initially when the New Zealanders occupied the camp in 1914 they

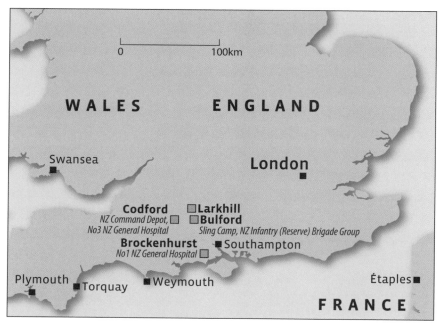

Map of important WW1 sites for the NZEF, southern England.

were there to build the quarters that would house the expected New Zealand troops en route to England. However, those troops were diverted to Alexandria; the New Zealanders who had joined the war in London were also sent to that theatre of war. When the New Zealanders reoccupied the camp site in 1916, it was known as Anzac Camp.[2] Over time the name reverted back to Sling Camp.

It was from Sling Camp that many New Zealand soldiers marched to war. Sling Camp was also the destination that most Category A battle-fit soldiers returned to at the end of the war.

As the war progressed other camps were opened and staffed, mainly for specialised training. But it was Sling Camp and the surrounding Salisbury Plain area that most New Zealand soldiers were familiar with through their route marches and training exercises.

The training at Sling was harsh and uncompromising right from the start.

Dave Dewar, a butter maker from the South Island, wrote home from Sling Camp in February 1917, saying that he used to think they were hard worked in the camps in New Zealand but that it wasn't a patch on Sling.

There is no use parading sick here unless you are dying. They won't take any notice of one. I am thankful to say I am in no need of the doctor yet. A terrible lot of our chaps are suffering with their feet. Nearly everyone is limping. The ground is frozen solid and as hard as granite and as we do a lot of walking it gives them fits. We had a fast ten-mile route march on Wednesday and they were dropping out all along the road. But I suppose they will get used to it.[3]

Dave Dewar also notes that the New Zealand officers had it as hard as the ordinary soldier did, commenting, 'Even our officers who came over with us are as ignorant as ourselves and are marched around in great style by corporals and sergeants. Don't we have a good grin when we see them and don't they look sheepish?'[4]

Like most Sling Camp soldiers, Dave Dewar makes comments about the brutal February weather the soldiers experienced. 'The cold is still intense but we don't feel it so much now. It never thaws here — freezes day and night and as we had a fall of snow on Sunday, of course it is still on the ground and likely to remain there.'[5]

As soldier Gordon Neill puts it, 'the discipline in Sling was intensive. It is with the British Army. Fortunately it is not with our people; our people in New Zealand are more humane.'[6]

Dave Dewar had a different understanding of the training conditions. He may not have liked it but he contrasted it to the training he had undergone in the New Zealand camp, which he called a farce by comparison. He felt that three months' thorough training in Sling Camp would produce very fine soldiers.

And that was the point of the tough regime followed at Sling Camp. There was much to be taught in the brief weeks before leaving for France.

George Jenkins, 1917.

Modern warfare had different demands of the men and their officers from previous military conflicts. Thousands of new recruits had to become part of a giant international fighting machine. They had to understand their roles, and be fit and disciplined in often a very short time.

George Jenkins writes in February 1918 that he is 'enjoying it [Sling Camp] as well as can be expected'. He further comments that 'training is not quite so strenuous as it was before as they were overdoing it and the result was they were ruining the men instead of making them fit'.[7] His next comments surprisingly escaped the censors' editing but they must have given his family pause for thought on their farm in the northern part of the North Island. George notes that 'Even now there are a lot of fellows dying. There has been a death pretty well every day lately and one day last week there were five men died and there is going to be an enquiry into it.'[8]

George was right. In February 1918 alone, twenty-nine men died in Sling Camp.[9] Four died on 13 February 1918 and one the day previously. Many of those soldiers were recent recruits from the 1917 reinforcements. Twenty-four soldiers died of measles with associated broncho-pneumonia complications. Other men had an assortment of illnesses including meningitis, scarlet fever and influenza, sometimes with a combination of the infections.

George explained to his family that there was going to be an enquiry into the reasons behind the deaths. In the same letter George notes the number of men in the camp was at 6000, and that the weather was unseasonably warm for February.[10]

In his letters written in 1918 George Jenkins reassures his father that he keeps in good health but that food was in short supply in England. He comments that often the soldiers refused to leave the mess room until they got more bread. George warns that he feared there would be a riot if rations were reduced any further. He observed that although over a 1000 soldiers had left for France, the camp was being readied for the new 33rd Reinforcements, which would push the numbers back up to 6000 again. George was looking forward to his draft leave after his training for the Western Front was complete and before he was sent to France.

Lieutenant Drew described the bull ring at Sling Camp where the soldiers practised their warfare skills. He tells of its 'bare slippery surfaces, its bleak winds sweeping across, its snow-covered rifle ranges' and the monotony of the repetitive military tasks the soldiers had to perform daily.[11] The bull-ring was 'worn bare of turf by the feet of nearly 100,000 New Zealanders' who trained there during the course of the war.[12]

Sling may have been the right choice as a training and toughening up base before soldiers went to the Western Front, but after the war the last thing on the troops' minds was more route marches and drills. They yearned for home. They did not want the harsh reality of army life. They craved a normal life.

What they got was a relentless diet of army discipline, including route marches, accompanied by compulsory education classes six days a week to prepare them for civilian life.

Routine Order 50 for the 27 February 1919 detailed the forthcoming March weekly timetable for troops. Soldiers in both Sling and nearby Larkhill Camps had similar daily routines of an hour-long route march, vocational classes and some form of physical activity to occupy them until 4 p.m. In the same set of orders officers were reminded to have one officer at the rear of the route march to prevent straggling. No smoking was permitted on the march.[13]

At home in New Zealand it was summer. By contrast at Sling Camp the weather was bitterly cold, wet and bleak. The soldiers' consistently recorded in their diaries the weather conditions they experienced at the camp.

George McLaren from the Auckland Regiment writes that the weather at Sling during late December 1918 and early January 1919 was 'miserable, cold and wet'.[14] On 5 February he records that it snowed. Official weather records support George's account. February 1919 was an unseasonably cold month, with temperatures below normal. In March it was cold and wet, with sleet and snow. April wasn't much better, with constant rain, lower than usual temperatures and fewer sunshine hours than normal.

Sling was organised differently from other military camps. The camp complement was divided into four separate battalions — Canterbury (No. 1), Otago (No. 2), Wellington (No. 3), and Auckland (No. 4). Otago and Canterbury battalions were sited at the base of Beacon Hill at the back of the camp, and Wellington and Auckland near to the front entrance. Each battalion was a separate camp with its own cluster of huts, training staff, headquarters and lieutenant-colonel in charge. The whole camp was controlled by a group headquarters presided over by the brigadier and his support staff. At the end of the war Brigadier-General Stewart was the General Officer Commanding (GOC) all Group A men from the various battalions stationed at Sling Camp.

In February 1918 when Sling started to bulge at the seams with men, an overflow camp was set up at nearby Larkhill. The high death toll from the measles epidemic and the subsequent enquiry referred to by George Jenkins in his letter home that same month gave additional reasons for a separate camp being established.[15] A memo written by the Surgeon-General from Southern Command on 21 February 1918 indicated that Larkhill, now referred to as No. 4 Camp, had been earmarked for new troop arrivals from New Zealand. However Larkhill was used as an isolation camp for the measles epidemic until June 1918.[16]

So in essence the repatriation centre encompassed men from both Sling and Larkhill Camps, along with troops stationed at Codford Camp about 25 kilometres (15.4 miles) west of Sling Camp who were fed progressively into Sling Camp as troops left for embarkation ports around Great Britain.

After the Armistice, as the men were transported back to Sling from different locations across Europe, it took some time for their mail to catch up with them. Often the news from home intensified their feelings of displacement. Many soldiers had indicated on their attestation forms that they were supporting other members in their family — often younger siblings or elderly parents. Now they felt they were needed at home, not in some godforsaken camp in the middle of a windswept and freezing cold plain. Not now that the enemy had been beaten.

Francis Payne Townsend was based in Codford Camp in early January 1919. He kept a diary where he reflected on life after the war. In his flowing penmanship that often ran over a number of calendar dates he describes his thoughts and experiences. He records the fact that he had little money, no leave and had just survived a 'dynamite march to Codford'[17] from Sling Camp.

His life changed on 19 January 1919. Townsend got a severe shock when he received a cable after church parade bluntly stating 'Father died 26th Dec'.[18] He was bewildered at this news: 'I can't make it out at all,' he writes, 'It seems plain enough but I can't help thinking it means grandfather. Am hoping it is so and am anxiously waiting more mail to get an idea of what is likely to be the case.'[19] Townsend badgered the post

Sling Camp, Charles E H Putt, 1919.

office and a week later he got his accumulated mail from New Zealand dating back to November 1918.

From this he learned that his father had died of heart trouble. He reflects in his diary that he thought that it might have been the 'Influenza which has apparently been raging in New Zealand for some time' that killed his father. He writes, 'Poor old dad I wish I'd been home before he went.'[20]

Tragedy upon tragedy unfolded for him in the next few days. Not only had his father died but also his grandfather. He then found out that good mates whom he had thought had left for home had been killed in

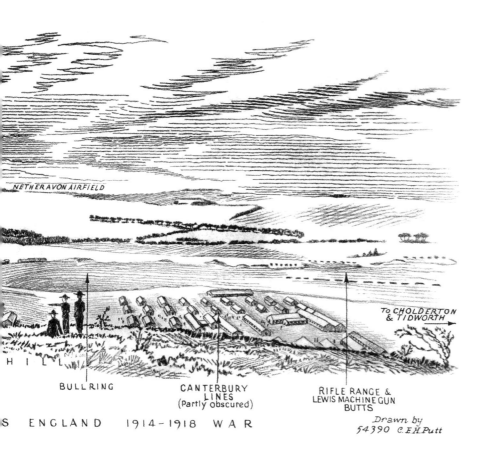

NETHERAVON AIRFIELD

To CHOLDERTON
& TIDWORTH

HILL

BULLRING
CANTERBURY
LINES
(Partly obscured)
RIFLE RANGE &
LEWIS MACHINE GUN
BUTTS

S   ENGLAND   1914-1918   WAR

Drawn by
54390 C.E.H.Putt

the final stages of the war. He was bereft.

There is anguish in his written lines; 'All my old pals are gone now. For what? It makes me wonder if it's all been worth it. Let's hope the world has finished with war forever.'[21]

The bad news continued as information trickled in from home about the influenza pandemic. Townsend pored over the published newspaper records of home casualties enclosed in letters sent to him. He notes the deaths.

While he is managing his grief he holds a running commentary on the rumours flying around the camp about the boats that are supposed

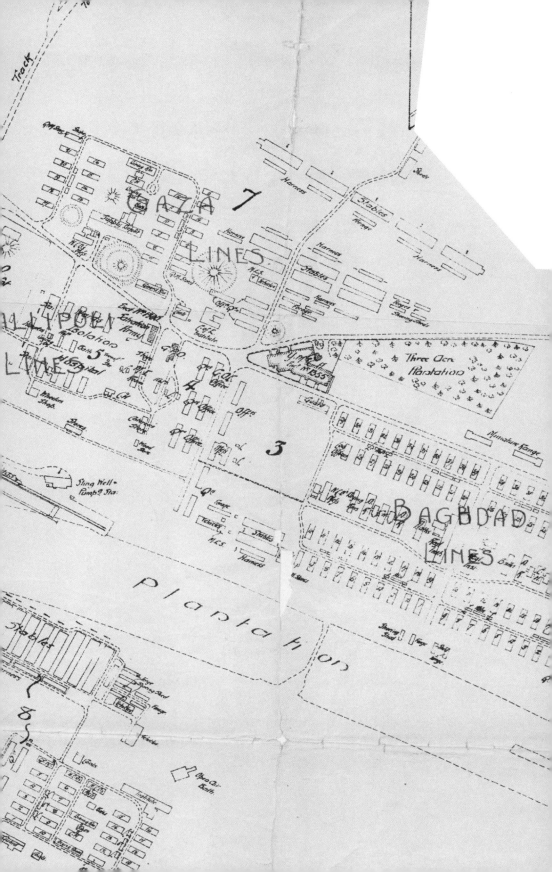

Map of Sling Camp, Eastern End, 1921

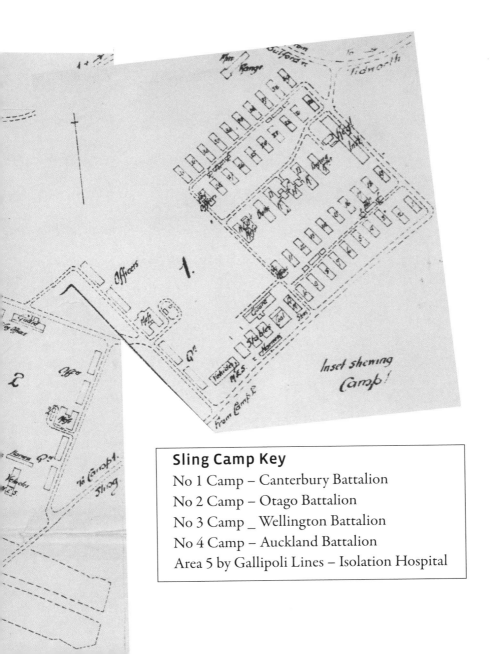

Sling Camp Key

No 1 Camp – Canterbury Battalion

No 2 Camp – Otago Battalion

No 3 Camp _ Wellington Battalion

No 4 Camp – Auckland Battalion

Area 5 by Gallipoli Lines – Isolation Hospital

to be taking them home. He now knows that due to labour unrest in Britain he is unlikely to get away any time soon. The anticipated sailings have been cancelled. He writes that the only soldiers leaving are the miners and hospital ships: 'We may be delayed some months. In addition there is talk floating about that New Zealand's allotment of ships is well below expectations.'[22]

Thousands of soldiers were confined to camp, with very little to occupy them apart from the monotonous army routines and some compulsory educational options, supplemented by a continuous flow of news from home, rumours and speculation to fill up their day. At the same time they were dealing with their own personal war traumas.

Townsend notes on 24 February 1919, '. . . another good pal gone west. Who is left and when will we hear of the last of it? This is depressing news.'[23]

Soldiers like Bert Stokes had also written about losing their friends, often at the time of their death. But sitting in camp hearing of others dying in the last stages of the war, the men must have thumbed back through those pages in their diaries where they had scrawled words of grief and despair. Bert Stokes filled pages in his war diary describing the depth of distress he felt when his great mate Reg Blackburn died in April 1918. He pours his heart out, emotions binding the words that describe his sense of loss.

I cannot realise he has gone under in the great battle and it is hard to believe I won't see him again on this earth. Oh I can't say how I feel. Reg was a brother to me. I always looked forward to meeting him because we knew each other and I could talk to Reg as I could not to anyone else in France. How we used to yarn of home, of loved ones, of our own dear land which he will now see no more. Now he has gone, given his life for his native land, for NZ. But while I think of my loss I too remember those whose hearts will be broken by the sad news — his mother and father, sisters, brothers and too the little girl whom he loved. My thoughts are far away across the seas — in N.Z. and I pray that God will comfort the broken hearted in their great sorrow.[24]

Bert and his friend Perc spent time looking for Reg's grave in the mud of France, and again Bert lets his words reveal the depth of his misery.

My eyes filled with tears as I knelt by the side of the grave. Strong as a man is in war and hardened as he gets to the everyday sights and grimness of it all my strength forsook me. I loved him as a brother, he fought bravely, he died nobly and now he lies at rest in the little village of Beaussart.[25]

So men like Bert Stokes and Francis Townsend and hundreds more with similar experiences were now fairly safe in Sling Camp, assured of getting home, while their friends remained behind in graves scattered across Europe and beyond. How those soldiers managed their pain appears to have been quite private, but they must have longed for home, recognising and no doubt hoping that a return to some kind of a normal life would help their recovery process.

Those men would have observed that within Sling Camp the detailed proposals for repatriation did not appear to be going to plan. Soldiers started to fear that the delays in shipping meant that the system announced to all the men wasn't in fact being adhered to; rumours and hearsay no doubt fuelled their discontent and built disquiet. Official announcements were distrusted and in turn reinforced their sense of helplessness.

Francis Townsend was perplexed by the numbers of early recruits who were still in camp. Men who had joined up early in the war were still waiting for their transport back to New Zealand. He confirmed his concerns about getting back home by observing that men in camp with him were from the 'employment companies, for instance, a large number of them are main body and early reinforcement men too which confirms the rumour that few boats are getting away at present'.[26]

On 1 March 1919 he notes, 'It was announced to us on parade today that the arrangements have been dislocated — no boats in February and none until the middle or end of this month.'[27]

A few days later, on 6 March, a new story surfaced. Townsend writes about rumours of 'improvement in the boat allotments and several boats said to be going shortly. All last month's allotment of 16–17 boats are said to be sailing this month.' He adds pragmatically, 'But it is too good to be true.' Townsend merely records that 'General Richardson says all away by July.'[28]

One rumour was true — that 2500 men would be moved to Sling Camp from Codford on Friday 7 March 1919. Once settled in Sling Camp, now overflowing with 6000 men,[29] Francis Townsend observed that there were as many men still in Sling Camp as when he was there previously. 'No boats since the *Hororata*, middle of January. Until today the 1914 North Island crowd marched out at 6 a.m. for Southampton. South Island boat in few days otherwise no sign of more boats till next month.'[30]

Outsiders realised the problems Sling Camp and its soldiers were facing. An offer of help was made to the New Zealand Army by Irven Willis Raymond, the chairman of the NZ War Contingent Association and the Red Cross, who was based in London. In his publication *New Zealanders in Mufti 1914–1918*, Raymond states that he and no doubt others knew that Sling Camp was congested, and that the men were restive. He writes that he knew what was likely to happen and that he stated his views to General Headquarters as 'strongly' as he could. Raymond's offer was to provide 2000 men the money they needed to go on leave for a fortnight. His offer was refused and within a fortnight of that refusal the two-day disturbance occurred. Raymond states quite clearly that in his mind if his offer had been accepted the riot could well have been averted, but instead £10,000 worth of damage was inflicted on property within the camp.[31]

It is not known whether Raymond's offer was ever put to those in charge of Sling Camp but no doubt they all pinned their hopes on the shipping stalemate being resolved quickly and the men sent on their way home.

Instead, an additional challenge presented itself.

Early in February 1919 and continuing through to March, a second bout of influenza struck the camps. Sling Camp was an ideal breeding ground. Many men were unwell. The weather was cold, wet and dreary. Troops were confined inside and in large numbers. The virus was contagious before it was diagnosed and so it quickly spread.

The men, survivors of the harshest of wars, fell sick, and in both Codford and Sling Camp, they started to die.

Soldiers who were newly arrived in the United Kingdom in 1918 were the worst affected. Those soldiers back from long periods at the Western Front appeared to have greater immunity to the virus. The influenza struck in two waves. The first outbreak was from late August 1918 until the end of that year and men were affected more particularly in Britain than in France.[32]

In October 1918 senior officers had tried to prevent the spread of the pandemic as much as they could by isolating camps and hoping that vaccination against the virus would protect the men but still they died.

From the start of 1919 the pandemic swept the United Kingdom for a second time. The men awaiting repatriation were unaware that the second wave of the virus had a lower mortality rate. All they knew was that they were getting letters from home listing the names of those who had died from influenza and they in turn were exposed to the epidemic yet again. They felt like sitting ducks with nowhere to go.

In total, from the Armistice in November 1918 until June 1919, twenty-two men were buried at Tidworth Cemetery. They were predominantly from the Sling Camp area. In Codford, thirteen New Zealand soldiers are laid to rest in the special cemetery dedicated to World War I soldiers. All died of influenza, pneumonia or complications from serious chest infections.

Over those first months in 1919 the soldiers' belief that the New Zealand Army Headquarters would get them home promptly was seriously undermined by the lack of shipping available to the Category A men.

Rumours flourished, were embellished and re-circulated. Reports of disturbances and demands by other Dominion soldiers in nearby camps took hold. The process of drafting men back to New Zealand did not appear to be fair. Frustrations surfaced, and discipline became frayed. Fragmented communication lines were unhelpful and the late cancellation of boats bound for New Zealand undermined official broadcasts about the anticipated shipping schedule. Embarkation rolls were published then cancelled. Army routines and disciplines were challenged and flouted.

With nothing much to do but ruminate on the months since Armistice, soldiers would have totted up the negatives they had endured – the unpopular march to Germany, the delays in shipping, the injustice of the shipping lists, the lack of money for leave, influenza, the cold, harsh surroundings, the overcrowded camp along with their boredom and feelings of helplessness.

The final straw that sparked the soldiers' fury was the last minute cancellation of the sailing of the boat *Kia Ora*, due to take just on a thousand South Island soldiers home.

And on 14 and 15 March 1919 the soldiers at Sling Camp rioted.

~ Chapter Four ~

The Sling Camp Riots: March 1919

14 March 1919
Canterbury, Wellington and Otago have rioted at Sling and there is the devil to play [sic]. They smashed the Sgts and Officers mess to pieces. Auckland is standing fast.[1]

GEORGE MCLAREN'S DIARY

It was a potent mix — an overcrowded camp, few boats, foul weather, mundane routines and an influenza epidemic that threatened to snatch away a soldier's dream of returning home. The frustrations and grievances of the previous months which had been simmering throughout the camps, fuelled by rumours and speculation, eventually erupted into a full blown riot on 14 and 15 March 1919.

By the time Francis Townsend and the rest of the 2500 troops arrived at Sling from Codford a week before the riots, the soldiers occupying Sling were mainly from the Otago, Canterbury and Wellington battalions. Most of the Auckland detachment was based at nearby Larkhill Camp.

Ten days previous to the insurrection at Sling Camp, Canadian troops had rebelled at Rhyll Camp at Kinmel Park in North Wales. Newspapers covering the Canadian uprising stated that five men were killed and 23 were wounded.[2] According to a report from Brigadier-General Melvill, who had taken over the administration responsibilities for the NZEF, the British newspapers inaccurately reported that, 'As a result of the riot at Rhyll Camp six transports left the following week.'[3] Incorrect or not, that information deepened the ripples of discontent in the New Zealand camps and reinforced the hardening attitude of the New Zealand soldiers towards those in authority.

Soldiers waiting for a boat at Sling Camp knew the delays could go on for many more months. If the Canadians could get some action by rioting then so could they. Of course the consequences for what the army considered to be a mutiny were swift and harsh. Twenty-five Canadian soldiers were convicted and given sentences ranging from 90 days detention to ten years' imprisonment. By the time the Canadian Courts Martial were held and the findings were made public, it was too late — the New Zealanders had rioted.

The accuracy of the events that occurred over that two-day period differ according to the involvement of the men concerned, but all the accounts capture the intense frustration felt by the troops waiting for transport home.

Francis Townsend captured the deep dissatisfaction of the men as it spilled over into outright defiance and rebellion. He writes in his diary on Saturday 15 March, after noting that the *Kia Ora* — the boat intended for South Island soldiers — was not in sight,

> *. . . rioting and mutiny broke out throughout the camp on Friday, the mob wrecking all the canteens, stores and officers and sergts messes. Damage estimated at about £2000 which we will have to pay. General Stewart addressed crowd and took a party of delegates to London to put complaints chiefly about boats before HQ. On Sunday evening we learn every item agreed to by HQ and more boats promised. Crowd still rioting at Bulford mostly drunk. Will only stop when they are sober.*[4]

Bert Stokes did not write about those March riots at the time they occurred, but when he was interviewed 68 years later he recalled the reasons for them and how the men felt.

Brigadier-General Stewart standing in his car addressing rioters at Sling Camp March 1919.

That all blew up because you see you had thousands of men there, with nothing to do, there was no training taking place because the war was over, there was no leave and we were just there with nothing much to do and only wanting to get back to New Zealand.[5]

In Bert's view it was not a deliberate act.

A lot of chaps got into the canteen one night and, you know they were a little bit frustrated about not having leave and not getting back to New Zealand and nothing to do. They were drinking and they got a bit drunk and that's how it started and the barrels got rolled out of the canteen, and I can remember now — Brigadier Stewart — he was in charge of the camp. He stood up amongst all the men you know, and almost tears rolling down his face, and asked the men to be calm and as a result four or five were sent up to London to see General Richardson, who was the officer in charge of the New Zealand troops in England. And when they came back we were all granted four or five days leave.[6]

John Beveridge a New Zealand soldier from Wellington waiting to go home was in the thick of the riot. As he remembered the events, it unfolded in the following manner.

> *There was no ships there coming to bring us home and it was a riot, it lasted for a week. I wasn't a drinker but the drink was the trouble. You see troops got stuck into the bulk stores. There were big canteens in each of these camps, they were all joined together. But the riot lasted for about a week. Anyhow in the end General Stewart came along one day and said, if it didn't stop they would bring in troops from the Southern Command. Evidently officers' mess, everything was smashed up and even the bulk stores, they were pushing cases of whiskey and spirits out the windows to the crowd outside.*[7]

Beveridge recalled seeing Brigadier-General Stewart standing up in his motorcar on a small hillock appealing to the men to stop the riot, and a soldier was urinating against its wheel. It was an act of utter insolence.

So why weren't the ships leaving from the United Kingdom to take the troops home?

There were very few ships sailing due to strike action across Britain. Workers had taken matters into their own hands in an attempt to force the government to make changes to the demobilisation process and workers' labour conditions. The British Government understood very well what millions of demobilised soldiers looking for work would do to their unemployment figures. The government's demobilisation plan aimed to release individuals back into employment reflecting the needs of industry rather than on the length of service a soldier had done. The public immediately saw the injustice of the scheme and was increasingly irked by the cumbersome administration systems used. Soldiers and civilians alike protested. The troops waiting to demobilise feared that the government had other plans for them. The military hierarchy in Britain was enjoying its newly won status and was reluctant to let it go. New territories had been 'won' in the war and needed an on-going military presence, while in existing colonial outposts like India unrest was constantly simmering. The last thing the British troops wanted was to be posted overseas to India or Palestine; or back to Europe or Russia. Riots broke out in many British Army camps.

A new British government had just been elected at the end of 1918 and it immediately had to confront the mounting nation-wide criticism about the demobilisation plan. A chorus of disapproval resounded throughout the country — the press, citizens, returning troops and workers created an ongoing clamour of condemnation. For several months after Armistice was declared there were protests, demonstrations, civil disobedience and strikes from one end of Britain to the other. 'Demobilisation represented a new problem, precedents for which were completely lacking.'[8]

It was apparent that the British demobilisation plan was unworkable. As the returned soldiers were absorbed into the work force those men who had worked as their substitutes had been dismissed. By the end of January, it was reported in the United Kingdom that over 100,000 men had been laid off. With no realistic national solution to hand, more strikers joined the unofficial walk-outs until at the close of January 1919 over 172,000 people had withdrawn their labour.[9]

The strikes, many of which were centred on shipyards and ports, had an immediate impact on the availability of shipping to New Zealand.

Back in New Zealand families waited anxiously for the return of their men and national newspapers, which had been charting the progress of the labour unrest across the United Kingdom, reported on the spread of the industrial action.

Herbert Hart noted in his diary on 16 February 1919 that he was waiting for his ship the *Corinthic* to sail. His departure date was to have been two weeks earlier but because of the strikes he had no idea when the actual date would be. Hart commented that 'overseas troops are becoming greatly congested in their many camps, discontent is increasing. Coalminers are demanding more pay and shorter hours and threaten to strike on the 15th of March if demands are not granted.'[10]

Hart wrote that six other ships bound for New Zealand were in the same situation.

On 30 January 1919 the *New Zealand Herald* reported that the strikes in the United Kingdom were very unusual as they were not authorised by the trade union leaders.[11] It appeared that shop committees had decided that a stand should be taken to get better working conditions while returning soldiers were being absorbed back into the work force. Essentially workers wanted a shorter working week and increased wages. The strikes gained momentum and support from a broad cross-section of industries. The British Government was caught in an impossible position. It could not negotiate with the strike leaders as the industrial action was unauthorised and the Minister for Labour had to support the trade union executives. The subsequent industrial unrest was affecting the vital shipping that was needed to take the Dominion soldiers home.

A newspaper report in the *New Zealand Herald* dated 8 April 1919[12] wrapped up a series of events that had started in January and carried through to February. The report stated that General Richardson's scheme aimed for the repatriation of 10,000 men per month. It said that 18 vessels were on the waiting list to take New Zealand soldiers home, but only one had been able to leave thanks to the New Zealand troops themselves undertaking the necessary work to make it ready for the long sea voyage. The *Herald* also confirmed that Brigadier-General Richardson had been to see the strikers in January and pointed out that the New Zealand soldiers needed to get home for health and family reasons. He offered to supply troops to repair and load the ships themselves and added that the New Zealanders would be very reluctant to do anything that would disadvantage the cause of the strikers. The Strike Committee had promised to consider Richardson's concerns, but three weeks later nothing had changed.

In the same article the *New Zealand Herald* reported that in February 1919 Brigadier-General Richardson had met again with the strikers and appealed to their sense of comradeship, highlighting that the New Zealand troops had fought alongside British soldiers in the war.

Richardson had also added that after some weeks with no word from the Strike Committee there was a very real threat that his troops were of a mood that they might take matters into their own hands and refit the ships themselves.

The mood of the soldiers in Sling Camp on 14 March 1919 was that they had had enough. Six thousand men, one camp, no ships and a riot was a New Zealand Army Headquarters' worst nightmare.

Senior New Zealand officers were desperate to get the situation in Sling Camp under control. At the start of the disturbances Brigadier-General Stewart, commanding Sling Camp, invited the men to elect a delegation of twelve soldiers from Sling Camp to go with him to New Zealand Army Headquarters in London on 15 March. He requested that the men put their complaints in writing. When they arrived at the New Zealand Army Headquarters in London they discussed their grievances at a meeting with Brigadier-General Melvill, who had replaced General Richardson, along with other senior officers.[13]

The elected soldiers, seven of whom were non-commissioned officers, had a list of sixteen formal questions to put to the officers about not only the shipping schedule and the strikes, but also about the conditions at Sling Camp. It was obvious from the type of questions asked that despite group routine orders being disseminated throughout the camp, either the most basic of information about the repatriation orders wasn't fully understood by the men or, more likely, they didn't trust what they were told and needed to have it confirmed by senior officers in a face-to-face meeting.

At that meeting the Sling Camp representatives were informed that the industrial strikes were over and the ships would soon be moving again.[14] Officers attending that meeting explained to the delegates that a complicating factor was that much of the shipping then in use had been worked exhaustively during the war and was in need of a dramatic overhaul in order to be passed as fit for service. If a ship failed that test then further delays would occur as the British Ministry of Shipping, the Board of Trade and the Admiralty had control of all such scheduling arrangements.

It was formally minuted at that meeting that the ship *Kia Ora* had been ready to sail from a military perspective ten days prior to its cancellation. It developed engine trouble and the sailing was stopped, hence the South Island troops were delayed in leaving Britain. The New Zealand Headquarters' staff had been informed that repairs on the *Kia Ora* were being pushed ahead with all speed possible. Such boats were unable to be repaired quickly. Sometimes it took up to three months to make a ship seaworthy again.

It was noted by senior officers at the delegates meeting that Sling Camp at that time was holding 6000 men, and having so many men sitting idle while they awaited their sailing orders was not an option.[15] The officers conceded that Sling Camp was not an exciting place to be confined in, and the education classes were one way of taking away the monotony associated with waiting for a boat home. However, by the end of the meeting the Sling Camp representatives had won a number of important concessions. The six compulsory days a week of educational training was reduced to three days a week, but was still compulsory.

An interesting question was raised on behalf of a 'number of sergeants' at Sling Camp. Those sergeants wanted to know why the quota of soldiers for the ship *Remuera* had been reduced. The reasons why some men had priority over others was carefully explained to the delegates, but the fact remained that the official number of officers, other ranks and nurses sailing on the *Remuera* for the 17 March sailing totalled only 481. Yet the same ship carried 614 passengers in September 1919 on a return voyage to New Zealand.[16] The men knew the ships, and would have understood from reading the embarkation roll that it was carrying fewer people than its capacity. They were understandably perplexed as to why the full quota could not be reached, especially when the camp was overflowing with men. What the men didn't know was that while official lists stated 481 passengers were on board the ship, the actual passenger numbers were 744. The sergeants may have had a lot more questions to ask had they known that 60 civilians and 34 Air Force cadets were on board along with 144 wives and children of commissioned and non-commissioned officers.[17] At the very least the men would have wanted to know how the lists were managed, and who made the decisions about the precedence civilians had over returning long-serving soldiers.

The matter of 'going on leave' was also raised at the meeting. Men from the early reinforcements had delayed taking a berth back to New Zealand so they could see around Britain while they were there. Unfortunately by the time they were back in camp ready to embark on boats, the strikes had reduced the number of vessels available to sail. In addition, a soldier applying for leave had to prove he had enough money to cover expenses while away from camp. No savings, no leave. The camps were bulging with men wary of taking any leave in case the boats started moving again and their name was listed for embarkation. They did not want to miss any opportunity to go home.

The delegation discussed gratuities and clothing allowances once the soldiers returned to civilian life. The men were assured that General Richardson, who by then was on his way home, would take these matters up with the New Zealand Government on his arrival.

The men won small victories over the requirement to salute picquets,[18] the early consideration of 'hard luck' cases for early repatriation, the number of guards to be on duty at any one time, and the purchasing of additional food by the New Zealand Government for the benefit of those en route home, to supplement the rations on board. They were also promised that the original priority scheme would be quashed. All troops would return to New Zealand in their class according to when they joined up regardless of whether they were a married man or an apprentice, student or essential worker. In addition the deputation won the concession of better publicity of the departure times and any delays in boating schedules.

The elected representatives then returned to Sling Camp and the outcome of the meeting was made public.

On 18 March 1919 Brigadier-General Stewart issued routine orders for Sling Camp.[19] The twelve elected delegates who had gone to London to speak on behalf of the men in the camp were, at the men's request, appointed by Stewart as 'official conduits' to hear any grievances that men in the camp believed needed to be brought to the attention of senior officers.

On paper it looked like a smart move to have a liaison group elected by the men to bridge the gap between officers and men, and to ease the discontent felt by men in the camp, especially in cases where their commanding officer had left for New Zealand.

Perversely all of those 'Sling Dozen' were on their way back to New Zealand within a few weeks, regardless of the length of time they had served.[20] Five of these men left Sling on 27 March 1919, ironically on the *Kia Ora* — the very boat that had been passed as unfit to sail and which had in all probability fuelled the riots of 14 and 15 March.[21] Four more of the twelve men left the following day and the remainder were on their way to New Zealand by mid-April.[22]

On the one hand it appeared that it was a mark of conciliation by the military to establish an elected liaison group to feed concerns through to senior officers for their attention. On the other hand it seemed that there was every attempt to repatriate those very men back to New Zealand as speedily as possible.

But before the rest of the troops could sail for home, there was a reckoning to be held for the damage done at Sling Camp, and eight men to be held to account for mutiny.

~ Chapter Five ~

The Day of Reckoning:
March 1919

It is an ugly episode and is a black stain on the fair name that the New Zealanders won throughout the war.[1]

BRIGADIER-GENERAL STEWART, MARCH 1919

New Zealand soldiers had previously been involved in a disturbance at Sling Camp during the Armistice period on 11 and 12 November 1918, some five months before the Sling riots in March 1919.

A court of enquiry investigating this previous Armistice Day unrest was held on 10 December 1918.[2] Witnesses to the incident testified that a dance had been organised for the men outside in a square to acknowledge the Armistice. The event was not held inside due to the infectious nature of the influenza outbreak. Despite this concern, because of rain the celebrations had moved inside into various buildings. There was a mixture of New Zealand, Australian and British troops in attendance. All those giving evidence said that the groups of soldiers were generally good natured although it was noted that some items were stolen during the disturbance.

New Zealand officers attested that they had put arrangements in place on the day and entertainment was provided for the men at Sling Camp. New Zealand and Australian army staff concurred that they had not received any requests for assistance from the British-based Bulford Camp next door on the night of 11 November, where most of the disturbance appeared to be centred. Many affidavits stated that if officers from Bulford had requested help, it would have been provided.

After hearing statements from sixty-two witnesses the court concluded that poor communication and co-ordination coupled with a lack of foresight in planning for revelries had led to the disorder. British and New Zealand troops were each ordered to pay forty per cent of the costs of the damages and the Australian troops twenty per cent. There was an admonishing of senior officers, with a comment that they had been lax in their attention to duty.

By contrast the later riot at Sling Camp on 14 and 15 March 1919 revealed a depth and scale of widespread defiance by enlisted soldiers rarely, if ever, seen before in New Zealand's military history.

It was not only the rioting men who staunchly refused to follow senior New Zealand officers' orders; the rest of the soldiers in both Sling and Larkhill Camps disregarded orders to assist officers in quelling the rioters and safeguarding property. This insubordination was most notable on the first day of the riot. Possibly the troops did not understand the gravity of the situation and dismissed it as a few men having a bit of fun and fooling about, with the officers' orders being an overreaction to the event. Certainly the recollections of men at Sling Camp at that time when they were interviewed years later indicated that it was a situation that got out of hand, inflamed by too much drink and a strong sense of injustice about the shipping delays and the perceived lack of fairness in the selection process for embarkation, as well as the troops' general feelings of frustration and boredom.

On that first day of the riots, 14 March, various orders were issued by officers relating to the protection of property. These orders were ignored by ordinary soldiers, reportedly, mostly in a genial manner. Even orders from a respected commanding officer were rebuffed.

Afterwards, the numbers of soldiers rioting may well have been assessed at a few hundred only, but it appears there was complicit agreement across both Sling and the nearby Larkhill Camp, particularly on the first day, that the remaining 5000 plus soldiers in those camps would not partake in any picquet duties against those who were actively involved in the riot.

Surprisingly, given the two days of riots and the extensive damage done to not only properties on the camps but also to the reputation of the New Zealand Army, only eight soldiers were arrested on a charge of mutiny. And of these eight charged, two were not convicted.

It is only by examining the testimonies of those giving evidence at the Court of Enquiry that a full picture emerges of what had happened on those two days of rioting.

It is important to note that at the time the Court of Enquiry was conducted, Brigadier-General Stewart was still in command at Sling Camp but he did not testify either personally or in writing.

The messages written by staff officers on his behalf to the British Southern Command in Salisbury on the first day of the disturbance give a sense of how the events had unfolded. Stewart stated that 200 men had raided two canteens at midday March 14. In an effort to calm the situation down, Brigadier-Stewart called meetings that same day with the Wellington Detachment at 2 p.m., the Canterbury Detachment at 2.15, finishing with the Otago men at 2.30 at their respective barrack squares and sent a memo out to that effect.[3]

Stewart paraded all the men and spoke to them at some length, and for much longer than originally planned, but the disturbance resumed again that night. In his messages to Southern Command, Brigadier-General Stewart outlined his orders to protect army property and noted that all rifles and ammunition had been secured in the armoury. The message revealed the extent of the damage to canteens and messes as well as the quartermaster's stores, and also refers to the activities of some Australian soldiers, VD patients from a nearby military hospital, who joined in the riot.

Stewart wrote a letter to his wife Nan a week after the disturbance. Its contents provide a sense of what happened from his perspective.

Understandably, Stewart was deeply affected by the incident. In his letter home, dated Saturday 22 March 1919, he confides to his wife that when he had written to her the previous week (after the riots) he had been in a 'very doleful strain' and that 'things in camp had gone very far astray and I was, in soldier's parlance, "fed up" with life.'[4] He then spells out the facts of the riots as he saw them. He refers to the lack of shipping and says that 'many of the men were disoriented and sullen', and he mentions the impact on the men of not having leave available to them, especially when they didn't have the savings to support themselves while away from the base.

He confirms that the riot had been inspired by the recent misreporting of the effect the Canadian soldiers' riots had had on getting more transports so that an increased number of those troops could be repatriated. By this time the strike action was coming to an end and some ships were leaving Britain. Stewart reveals that there were certain types of men in Sling Camp who thrived on rumours, and they had added fuel to the simmering discontent in the camp. He also states that there were men with criminal backgrounds who had used the riots to steal money under cover of the drinking binges the others were indulging in during the disturbances.

Stewart's overall analysis of the disturbance clearly would have added an important insight into the riots — an insight that was missing when the Court of Enquiry assembled five days after he wrote his letter home.

The British General Officer Commanding (GOC) the Southern Command ordered that the Court of Enquiry be convened on 27 March 1919. The president of the court was Lieutenant-Colonel G H Geddes C.B. Royal Field Artillery. Two New Zealand officers, Major Merton and Major Daldy from the New Zealand Expeditionary Force, were part of the five members of the Court.[5] Major Campbell represented the Australian Army, and Major Hardy and Major Bridges were from the British Imperial Army. The purpose of the Court of Enquiry was to investigate 'the extent of damage and loss at Sling and Bulford Camps by certain disturbances which occurred at Sling Camp on 14.3.19 and subsequently by which Units it is recommended same should be made good.'[6] The members of the court were to discover who was to blame and where the costs should fall for the damage to and loss of property.

A range of soldiers — including British and Australian officers, along with their New Zealand counterparts — gave evidence under oath to the Court of Enquiry.

Major R A R Lawry from the Canterbury Regiment, the staff officer in charge of Administration 'A' Group NZEF, was the first witness at the enquiry. He attested that the continual delay in troopships home affecting the Otago and Canterbury detachments had fired up the frustration and anger of the men, who had not had a boat home since 1 February that year. At the beginning of his testimony to the court Lawry commented that the first ship since February was in fact leaving that very day when the court sat, 27 March 1919.

He reported that on the day of the riots in March 1919 senior officers who appeared to understand their men's underlying complaints were actively trying to address those grievances. It also appeared that the riot came out of nowhere. Lawry said, 'The staff had no reason to anticipate any destructive outburst.'[7] However it appeared that with the postponing of the departure of yet another boat the temper of the men, especially those from the South Island, was set at ignition point.

According to Lawry's evidence, at approximately 2 p.m. on Friday 14 March the South Island troops had streamed onto the Wellington parade ground where General Stewart was talking to the troops about a number of complaints they had. There was obviously a list of concerns, and Stewart knew that the answers to those questions would be complex and detailed. He had asked the men to put their concerns in writing. Stewart had got to the stage where the Wellington troops had agreed to be part of a plan to elect twelve men from Sling Camp to go to London to voice their grievances to senior officers at Headquarters and for the Wellington troops not to undertake any further action. On account of that, Stewart won the same compromises with the Canterbury Detachment later in the day at his 4 p.m. meeting with them. Lawry does not mention the Otago contingent's response to Stewart's offer.

Something appears to have united the various detachments'

individual complaints and brought them together for a common purpose of venting their combined frustration and anger at the on-going shipping delays. Stewart's offer of elected delegates to communicate the troops' dissatisfaction with the current repatriation arrangements to Headquarters' staff in London did not placate the intensity of feelings and resentment in the wider group. Once the various forces combined, the gravity of the situation escalated and whirled out of control.

Lawry had received information that led him to believe more trouble would follow. He tried to follow orders to get a picquet of 150 men to protect the Group Canteen bulk store. However, as he explained to the court, 'owing to the general disaffection of the men, commanding officers reported that they were unable to secure a picquet'.[8] It was total defiance by his men. They might not be rioting themselves but they were not going to participate in actions arising from orders to defend property. Within half an hour the store he was endeavouring to safeguard had been stripped bare. Lawry reported seeing between twenty and thirty Australian soldiers, many dressed in hospital blue uniforms, mixing in with the New Zealand troops. He told the court that there were about six Australians in khaki, who were very drunk. By this time the riot was in full swing with a number of stores being looted by soldiers.

Acting on instructions from Brigadier-General Stewart, Lawry again sent orders out to all commanding officers to protect their camps. In addition, Lawry tried to raise three picquets with six officers per picquet and 200 men (in total 18 officers and 600 men) to go to the neighbouring Bulford Camp to protect property there. He was unsuccessful. The men refused to comply with the order. He sent out patrols of officers instead.

According to Lawry's statement there were only about 200 or so New Zealanders rioting but a large number of troops were looking on and a great deal of noise came from the crowd, which in turn attracted more spectators. Later that evening the officers' messes in numbers 1, 2 and 3 camps were broken into by the men. Lawry testified, 'No troops could be obtained to quell the disturbance.' While rioting in that section of the camp had subsided by about 9 p.m., an hour later it was reported that the quartermaster's stores in number 3 camp had been raided and, as Lawry put it, 'cleaned right out, and all stores removed'.[9] As far as Lawry was concerned the rest of the night was uneventful.

Lawry testified to the court that on the following day, Saturday 15 March, he addressed 400 troops in the YMCA building at Sling Camp and asked them to go to Bulford Camp. This time he was more successful. It seemed that the soldiers may have interpreted the previous day's events as a bit of a lark, but when it carried over to the following day they finally understood the seriousness of what they were dealing with.

On the afternoon of 15 March New Zealand troops accompanied officers to Bulford Camp to stop soldiers from destroying more property there. Patrols of officers and sergeants were on duty in the Bulford area and in the nearby town of Amesbury until 11 p.m. that evening. Lawry also had to be vigilant the following day when he was given reports of men intending to raid stores at Bulford and Amesbury railway stations. This time he had the full support of his men and any attempts to break into the buildings were thwarted.

The second witness at the Court of Enquiry, Lieutenant-Colonel Mead, the commanding officer of the Canterbury Detachment, gave a concise account of the actions with which he was involved.

Mead explained that the discontent of the soldiers was expressed at the parade to attend compulsory education at about 10.15 a.m. on Friday 14 March. Then, at 11.45, an estimated 300 men went to the guard room and released three prisoners. Mead with another officer went to a canteen about to be raided by New Zealand soldiers. When the door was smashed open and over fifty men surged into the canteen, Mead ordered them to leave; but they defied his command and took five barrels of beer. More officers arrived in support and with their help Mead was able to shut the men out of the store. While Mead reported to Brigadier-General Stewart, the remaining men guarded the canteen with instructions that should the men return for more beer they were to run the remaining barrels dry. The men did return and the barrels were emptied by the officers.

Orders flew thick and fast across Sling Camp. It is difficult to establish just how many soldiers from the ordinary ranks complied with the direct orders from senior officers.

On the surface, when looking at the cables detailing the orders that had been given by Stewart, it appeared as though he and the other officers had the situation under control. What the Court of Enquiry determined was that, in fact, the soldiers refused to obey Stewart's commands. General Stewart had asked detachment officers to picquet their own lines with 'good men'. It appears from the consistency of the affidavits supplied to the court, that no ordinary soldier obeyed orders on the first day of the riot.

In his 22 March letter home to his wife in New Zealand Stewart said that in his view the seriousness of the riot was underpinned by the fact that 'many sergeants and corporals were among the rioters and the Officers could get no body of men to join in knocking out the ringleaders'.[10] It appeared that the ordinary soldier's loyalty was split between commissioned and non-commissioned officers. For that first long day soldiers refused to obey Stewart's orders.

Stewart recorded in his letter that he had indeed arranged for a meeting with the Wellington Detachment at 1.45 p.m. on 14 March 1919 to talk about another matter but was 'speedily surrounded by a mob of nearly 2000 with many beer drunks and with excitement in the forefront'.[11] He had taken his car around to the parade ground in order to stand on the seat so he could be seen, but the car was attacked over a ten-minute period and he thought it would be wrecked, no doubt with him in it. Interestingly Brigadier-General Stewart referred to a strike agitator in his letter home and he revealed that it was this soldier who came to his aid, quietening down the crowd and allowing him to speak to the men, explaining the current situation and answering questions for nearly two hours.

Given the lack of support from the troops and the involvement in the riots by a group of non-commissioned officers, the remaining officers came up with a plan to find out what exactly was happening. The Court

General Stewart addressing the rioters at Sling Camp in March 1919. He refers to the soldier beside him as 'the strike agitator'.

of Enquiry heard that officers from the Wellington Detachment had borrowed privates' uniforms, and mixed freely with the rioters and the crowd in order to discover any intelligence that would help them resolve the disorder.

In his witness statement, Second Lieutenant Donald from the Wellington Detachment advised the court that he was disguised as a private at the Wellington Officers' Mess when the nearby canteen supply store was rushed by New Zealand soldiers. When he got closer to the building he saw twenty to thirty Australian soldiers dressed in hospital blue uniforms from the nearby VD hospital mingled in with them. The looters inside the building passed out items to the men waiting and the goods were taken away. The crowd then went from building to building where there might be any items of interest they could take. Donald was in the company of two other officers, and they tracked Australian troops who were carrying kit bags full of looted goods back to their hospital. They saw them climb the fence and get back into the hospital grounds.

They then alerted the hospital authorities. Donald's evidence was corroborated by Australian officers' statements.

Brigadier-General Stewart had issued orders during the riot to all officers asking them to persuade the rioting soldiers to stop their looting rather than to use force. All men in picquets were armed with entrenching tool handles. No rifles were to be used. The officers at the camp were totally outnumbered and any attempt to force the men to acquiesce through the use of arms would have created a much worse confrontation and possibly bloodshed, as had occurred in the previous Canadian riot. Even armed with trenching tools, the officers were no match for the men.

Lieutenant Morey of the New Zealand Engineers, in his sworn statement, revealed that on 14 March a stand-up fight broke out between the men and officers in front of the Wellington Officers' Mess. The men overpowered the officers and surged into the mess, looting the bar and smashing windows.

Australian officers based at the nearby hospital admitted that some of their patients were involved in the unrest but informed the court that it was the New Zealand soldiers who cajoled patients out of the wards and enticed them to the perimeter of the hospital with offers of looted food, drink and cigarettes. The Australian witnesses stated that they had ordered the patients back into the hospital and that all the patients were in bed and accounted for when the final roll call was made. Australian officers patrolled the grounds and the wider camp area, ordering any patients back to the hospital. All pilfered goods in their possession were returned to the New Zealand Army on 27 March.

Stewart's British counterpart at Bulford Camp, Colonel Lloyd, did give evidence at the Court of Enquiry. His detailed statement at the court highlighted the complete breakdown in authority that had spread throughout not only Sling Camp on 14 March but had also filtered through to Larkhill Camp where the Auckland Detachment was stationed. Lloyd told the court that he was asked by General Stewart to provide transport to collect men from the Auckland Detachment based at the nearby Larkhill Camp to be picquets in Bulford Camp, as Stewart was unable to get any men from Sling Camp to comply with his orders. Colonel Lloyd's statement is brief and to the point: 'Ten lorries were at once despatched and returned empty.'[12]

The message from this was clear. The soldiers were standing fast against all officers' orders to be part of any reinforcement and protection squad.

Despite the gravity of the situation, the orders from both New Zealand and the British Imperial Army hierarchies were very specific; there was to be no use of force. The fall-back position was to get rid of any remaining liquor and to secure buildings as the men left them to prevent any further ransacking taking place. Colonel Lloyd made the comment that from his perspective throughout the whole episode the New Zealand soldiers were for the most part good natured and there was no violence.

Lieutenant Morey was in Bulford Camp, and just as he was on the brink of talking the New Zealanders out of looting a building, the Australian soldiers who were mixed in with the crowd of troops refused to comply with his request. The soldiers then combined forces and the lower floor was stripped. Imperial soldiers joined in the ransacking. Eventually Morley was able to contain the building, and once a picquet appeared he had no further trouble.

By the following day, Saturday 15 March, the tenor of the disquiet had changed. On the second day, it appears that the majority of the troops realised that it was far more serious than a few soldiers letting off steam and moved to support the officers in their attempts to control the looting and ransacking of the camp.

The Court of Enquiry heard sworn statements from thirty-two witnesses. The court then decreed that it had read the statements from further witnesses who were available to testify and felt that any further evidence submitted would not alter the opinion that it had formed. The remaining affidavits all contained additional material about the riots, including statements illustrating the involvement of Australian troops.

Next the New Zealand Army turned its attention to the eight men imprisoned and facing a court martial for offences committed during the Sling riots.

– Chapter Six –

Restitution: April 1919

The whole of the old world is full of unrest and it will take some talking to get all steadied down again. All history records that excesses come when armies are being demobilised and we have to look for it after the 1914/1918 war.[1]
BRIGADIER-GENERAL STEWART IN A LETTER TO HIS WIFE, MARCH 1919

The district court martial was held at Devizes on 14 and 15 April 1919, exactly one month after the riot. It was presided over by Lieutenant-Colonel Sinel from the Auckland Regiment as president, and its members were Major Columb from the Wellington Regiment and Captain Thring from the Royal New Zealand Artillery. Eight men from Sling Camp were charged with mutiny.

The first charge against the eight men accused them of persuading soldiers in His Majesty's NZEF to join in the mutiny at Sling Camp on 14 March 1919 and inciting soldiers to mutiny by attacking officers' messes and other regimental buildings. The second charge was that those charged joined in the mutiny by combining with other soldiers to resist and offer violence to superior officers in the execution of their duty.

Only one of the accused soldiers' army records contains his full court martial details. The full account reveals that the same officers giving evidence against that one solider appeared as witnesses against other charged soldiers as well. All the other soldiers charged with mutiny have a brief outline of the court martial charges noted in their army records.

Six soldiers were convicted and two had their charges dismissed. All six soldiers were convicted only of the first charge.

Four of the convicted soldiers held the rank of sergeant, and two of them had been awarded medals for bravery just prior to the riots.

One such award was for 'conspicuous gallantry and devotion to duty' in October 1918. The soldier concerned had been recommended to receive a military medal for his assault on a German machine-gun crew, killing them all, but was ultimately awarded the Distinguished Conduct Medal only three weeks prior to the riot. His punishment for participating in the riot was to drop one rank, to corporal.

The second soldier had just been presented with the Belgian Croix de Guerre,[2] awarded by the King of Belgium. His citation revealed that he had been courageous, shown initiative and displayed great leadership to his section. He was sentenced to six months hard labour and reduced to the ranks. Ironically his award was noted in the *London Gazette* while he was being held in prison.

Three of the four soldiers with the rank of sergeant were reduced to the ranks.

Five of the six soldiers were imprisoned with varying sentences of hard labour. All the convicted men had been away from home a long time, one of the soldiers having been in the army for nearly five years at the time of the riots. Many had been injured and hospitalised over the years. All were South Island men.

All incomplete prison sentences were remitted on 4 July 1919. The men were released from Wandsworth Prison in London where they had been serving their sentences and were returned to New Zealand immediately.

A point had been made. Such insurrections would not be tolerated. Military regulations would not be flouted. Regardless, it seems inconceivable that only six soldiers were convicted from the hundreds of troops involved in two days of riots inflicting enormous damage to property and reputation.

The question also has to be asked as to why so many sergeants were ringleaders in the March disturbance and what effect did that have on the ordinary soldiers at Sling Camp during this unsettling period?

At the meeting with senior officers on 15 March 1919, the delegation of Sling soldiers on behalf of sergeants at the camp had asked why the quota of troops on board the *Remuera* had been reduced. This question was listed among others that queried the repatriation priorities of married men, apprentices and students on those rolls. It signalled an overall focus on what was possibly seen by long-serving troops as unmerited soldiers being given preference over them.

Brigadier-General Stewart had already reflected on the involvement of the sergeants in the riot when he wrote to his wife saying that the non-commissioned officers had had a strong influence on men not obeying their officers' orders.

Parts of the embarkation list for the *Kia Ora*, due to sail early in March 1919 and whose cancellation was the cause of the disturbance in Sling Camp, still exists. It is clear from those pages that a number of men had been moved up the list and repatriated out of turn. The remarks column on the embarkation list merely states 'G.O.C' (General Officer Commanding). Whether it was Stewart's own decision to add the new names out of turn or whether he was ordered to do so is not known.[3]

Although the numbers are not overwhelming, it is useful to compare the background of those earlier repatriated soldiers against the criteria for preferential repatriation. The work that the men on that embarkation list did prior to joining the army was mainly clerical. Few of the men were married. None appeared to be cases of extreme hardship. Most of the men were from either late 1917 or 1918 reinforcements. Therefore, given the nature of the rumours and speculation that abounded throughout the camp at the time, it is easy to see how the fact that a few men were enabled to return home 'out of turn' could suddenly grow in significance and become inflated out of all proportion. It does lend credence to the concerns the soldiers' elected representatives voiced when meeting senior officers during the disturbance.

Despite the fact that many of the Sling delegation's requests were agreed to in writing by senior officers at that pivotal March meeting in London it took some time before repatriation arrangements were changed.

Some of the comments raised by the Sling delegation about the unfair embarkation selection process to New Zealand resonated with senior officers well after the meeting on 15 March. Coded conversations were exchanged between New Zealand and London NZEF headquarters about the repatriation process.

On 4 April 1919 a cable was received in London from the Ministry of Defence in Wellington. The message stated that 'private cables indicate that nominations for priority in repatriation based on Efficiency Board recommendations are being declined'. It asked 'What is the position?' A coded response was sent back to New Zealand the same day. The cable indicated that the disturbance at Sling was the result of men being sent back out of order on the instructions of the first Military Service Board. The writer said that they considered it advisable to cancel such arrangements and asked if the recipient agreed.[4]

On 29 April Brigadier-General Melvill wrote a report about Sling Camp to the Ministry of Defence in Wellington, and presumably to Minister of Defence Sir James Allen. In his report Melvill expanded on the discussions held with the delegation of men from Sling Camp on 15 March 1919, parts of which appear to be informal and not to have been minuted. The men had informed Melvill that one of their main grievances was that very late reinforcements to the war were being repatriated back to New Zealand due to political influence and recommendations from the National Efficiency Board. Melvill sought the minister's support to put a stop to the interference.[5]

Sir James Allen was also concerned about the soldiers' deeply held resentment with men returning out of the order set out in the demobilisation categories and strove to get to the bottom of the issue.

In a cable sent to the NZEF Headquarters in London on 29 April 1919 he tested a set of theories as to what had made the waiting troops so disgruntled with the repatriation process. Sir James Allen summarised the repatriation arrangements made in New Zealand from the time hostilities stopped. He explained that the military service boards had been disbanded. He outlined the establishment and role of the National Efficiency Board that investigated all applications out of the 'normal sequence' for returning soldiers. He asked if it had been fully explained to the men that soldiers were only returned out of sequence if a case of extreme hardship had been made. Sir James then asked if men had been returned out of order due to recommendations from New Zealand or if, as he suspected, authorities in Britain had 'ignored' large numbers of the board's recommendations. He claimed that there was evidence in New Zealand that this was in fact so.[6]

It was only after exchanges between Melvill in London and the Minister of Defence in Wellington at the end of March 1919 that the negotiated deal of all men being repatriated purely according to their enlistment date with no exceptions was brought into force.

At the same time the army was trying to understand the reasons for the riot and attend to its aftermath, it had to also turn its attention to making good the damages wrought in the two day disturbance, as per the directions from the Court of Enquiry. The court had found that ninety percent of the cost of the two-day riots should be proportioned to the New Zealand Army and ten percent to the Australian Army.

The court ruled that the total cost of the damages to property and equipment was calculated at £11,707.15s.2d. Of this the New Zealand Army was deemed responsible for £10,786.10s.2d and the Australian Army £921.5s.0d. The Australian Army disputed this analysis of the amount of damage their troops had incurred and contested the ruling. In the end the New Zealand Government paid the entire amount, relieving the Australian Army of any obligation to contribute.[7]

A problem arose when it was realised that the sum apportioned to the New Zealand Government was the full amount for all damages without separating out damage and losses to the British Imperial Army's property, as distinct from those incurred by the New Zealand Army for their own losses. The British Imperial Army pressed for all the costs awarded by the Court of Enquiry to be paid to it, regardless of what had been sustained by the New Zealand Army.[8]

Correspondence between the British Imperial Army, the New Zealand Army and the New Zealand Government passed back and forth for many months before the matter was finally settled. The New Zealand Army Headquarters in London and the Minister of Defence in New Zealand traded many coded telegrams trying to sort out where the responsibility to pay for the losses should fall.

The New Zealand Audit Office joined in the debate about the awarding of costs in August 1919, giving a strong direction to the New Zealand Government not to forward any payment to the British Government until that government made a claim detailing all the losses they had sustained and that the calculated amount be accompanied by a corresponding demand for compensation. The New Zealand Audit Office feistily challenged General Richardson's opinion that all the damaged huts at Sling Camp should be left in the same condition as when the New Zealand Expeditionary Force took them over. The Audit Office disputed the British Army's assertions that the huts were going to be used in the future, and advised that until any evidence was presented to the contrary the New Zealand Government should not pay any restitution.

A document itemising the losses of both armies was prepared for the New Zealand Military Forces in January 1920 by Brigadier Johnston, the officer in charge of New Zealand troops in the United Kingdom. The British Imperial Army property losses at Bulford Camp included a motorcycle, damage to buildings and assorted clothing. The document disclosed that the full amount to be paid to the British Government was £733.[9] The rest of the losses as determined by the court and revised by a more accurate reassessment of the true value of the damage were paid partially by the various regimental canteen accounts, with the New Zealand Government's public account paying the greater part of the damages of over £8,000. This was mainly for the loss of stock from the various quartermasters' stores and officers' messes.

Captain Harry Clark was responsible for repairing the damage done to the hutments at Sling Camp after the riots. In his diary he records that by using the skills of the soldiers based at Sling and sourcing material for the repairs from outside firms, in his estimation he saved forty percent of the overall costs for the New Zealand Army.[10]

In New Zealand, news of the riots had been delayed reaching the general population until the first shipload of soldiers from Sling returned home after the disturbance had taken place. In May 1919, an unnamed overseas correspondent penned a full report that was distributed to newspapers throughout the country. The *Ohinemuri Gazette* published that report on 14 May 1919 referring to the riots as 'The most serious riot in the history of the New Zealand Expeditionary Force'. The anonymous correspondent condemned the riots and commented that fortunately New Zealand's good name had not been tarnished by any reference to the riots in the British press.[11]

Brigadier-General Stewart reflected on the level of violence experienced during the riots and wrote the following lines to his wife:

The terrible thing was an ugly demonstration of passions uncurled and the devil in man. We have been training these fellows in blood lust and the will to kill and we are now in the aftermath. The whole of the old world is full of unrest and it will take some talking to get all steadied down again.[12]

As the men were 'steadied' down after the riots, and despite the army agreeing to ease up on some routines imposed on the impatient soldiers, the army hierarchy still faced a burning issue — even with the boats now sailing there were still thousands of men to be repatriated.

With the embarkation rolls under review and many men who had been involved in the March disturbance listed in the boats leaving for home, the men in Sling Camp appeared to settle down. However Brigadier-General Stewart had confided to his wife that after the riot relationships were strained, and it was difficult to get officers, NCOs and men to work together.[13] In April Brigadier-General Stewart was succeeded by Brigadier-General Young who sought to re-establish order and implement routines back into the camp with the remainder of the troops that were waiting to go home.

The camp buildings were under repair, the ships were moving again and most of the troops' grievances had been attended to, but it was now five long months after the Armistice had been declared, and the question still remained — What should be done with the waiting men still in Sling Camp?

— Chapter Seven —

Constructing the Kiwi: April–June 1919

Partly to keep the men employed, and also to commemorate the occupation of Sling Camp by the New Zealand Troops throughout the Great War, it was decided that an emblem of some description representative of New Zealand should be constructed in the Camp.[1]

FROM THE DIARY OF CAPTAIN HARRY CLARK

On 2 February 1919, a memo on behalf of Brigadier-General Stewart was been sent out to all officers leading the various New Zealand detachments within the camp.[2]

It contained a very simple request. Brigadier-General Stewart had selected a kiwi as the New Zealand emblem he wished to see carved into the chalk-based hillside behind the camp to mark the fact that thousands of New Zealand soldiers had trained at Sling and left for the Western Front from its gates. Stewart wanted to know if there were men in any of the New Zealand detachments who had the necessary skills to carry out the design and setting out work required to create the emblem.[3]

Negative responses came thick and fast from all detachments. According to the replies from senior officers, including the nearby Larkhill composite camp and the medical headquarters, there were no men available of sufficient skill to undertake the task.

At that point the idea of digging out a kiwi emblem on Beacon Hill seems to have been shelved as military minds focused on the more pressing challenge of securing enough ships to get the men back to New Zealand. By early February senior New Zealand officers knew they had a burgeoning crisis on their hands. If the striking port workers were not back at work within a very short time there would be unrest in the camps when the numbers of men in them swelled as more troops returned from France and Germany.

Why did Brigadier Stewart even consider a kiwi for an emblem? The selection of the kiwi by the military as an enduring emblem to leave behind was an interesting choice over other symbols associated with the New Zealand Expeditionary Force. The fern would have been a strong contender given the 'Fernlander' and 'Fernleaf' identities tagged to the New Zealand contingents, and the fern also appeared on many regimental badges.

The Second Canterbury Regiment had been using the kiwi on its badges since 1886, and throughout the duration of World War I the image of the kiwi bird became popularised as a uniquely New Zealand symbol beyond the military sphere. Part of the kiwi's increasing acceptance as a national icon was due to Trevor Lloyd, a cartoonist employed by the *New Zealand Herald,* who had been using a variety of images including the kiwi as points of reference for the New Zealand identity. Lloyd used the Kiwi from 1905 onwards to get across key ideas and traits of the colony's unique and robust characteristics in cartoon form.

Trevor Lloyd's kiwi cartoons showed the bird in a number of international situations that gained for him (and his newspaper) enormous popular reader appeal. Often the flightless ground-dwelling bird was pitted against sterner foe, and when the kiwi came out on top despite all the odds, it must have swelled the collective chests of the population with pride. It was a classic David and Goliath scenario showing that a smaller and possibly weaker country, represented by a dun-coloured flightless bird, could punch above its weight internationally and be immensely proud of its achievements.

The kiwi symbol was possibly also used by the New Zealand soldiers

Above: 'Britain defeated by the all Blacks', 1908 , by Trevor Lloyd, along with his drawings of kiwis, below.

themselves in a bid to positively distinguish them from their Australian counterparts. By the end of the war, the term 'Kiwi' and the symbol of the bird were well on their way to being accepted in the national psyche as representing not only the country but also the people, both individually and collectively.

After the riots of 14 and 15 March and the subsequent courts martial of the men charged with mutiny, the overall command of Sling Camp changed. Brigadier-General Stewart, a man in his early fifties who by this time had served overseas for more than three and a half years, particularly in France, was relieved of his position at Sling Camp. With the reduction in the number of compulsory education classes down to three days a week, the men remaining in the camp needed something to do to fill their time. The senior officers at Sling Camp had to re-think their position. While the idea of constructing a kiwi emblem to keep many men active and well-occupied had already been floated by Brigadier-General Stewart, the idea had not been tested as to its practicality.

Brigadier-General Young, who replaced Stewart in April 1919, may have decided to carry on with his predecessor's idea in the two-fold belief that it would provide a quick fix to occupy the men, take their minds off the recent riots and provide them with a sense of pride in creating a permanent record of their own and their fallen comrades' contributions to the war effort.

Major Lawry, who had been Brigadier-General Stewart's administration officer in charge of all communications from the brigadier's office across Sling Camp and who was now carrying out the same role for Young, knew of the original memo, as he had issued it. It is conceivable, given that Lawry and Stewart had worked closely together, that some discussion had been held between the two of them about the merits of leaving a New Zealand emblem behind.

Lawry belonged to the Second Canterbury Regiment and so would have been very familiar with the kiwi emblem, his regimental insignia. Once Brigadier-General Young assumed command of the camp, if any advocating was to be done in favour of the kiwi emblem representing

New Zealand being constructed on Beacon Hill, Lawry would have been in a strong position to push for it as an appropriate memorial.

It seems Brigadier-General Stewart's original kiwi idea was reviewed and adopted.[4] It was decided that the Army Education Unit would provide the necessary staff to plan the implementation of the project.

Apart from brigadiers Stewart and Young, three people in particular were involved with the construction of the kiwi on Beacon Hill. Sergeant Majors Percy Blenkarne and Victor Low were from the NZEF Education Unit and had particular skills relating to the task. Captain Harry Clark, the works and barracks officer for Sling Camp, had the construction experience required to organise the cutting of the kiwi into the hillside.[5] Together these men were responsible for the kiwi moving from being an abstract idea to becoming a design drawn on paper, being realigned to fit onto the designated site, and finally being dug out to the correct profile on the slopes of the hill.

Beacon Hill reared up from the base of Sling Camp to overlook the entire camp and was a prominent land feature on the Salisbury Plain. It was close to the Otago and Canterbury detachments' huts, which were at the rear eastern end of the camp. Once completed, the emblem would be clearly visible to everyone in the camp and beyond. It would be similar to other chalk figures carved into the hills around Southern England over the centuries. Beacon Hill was a near uniform slope of about ten degrees facing west. Symbolically, the face and beak of the kiwi emblem when finished would point towards the south — towards New Zealand and home.

Brigadier-General Young might well have thought the kiwi image could be put on the hill quite quickly, but there were a number of technical steps that had to be considered and managed before the actual construction work could begin, and it was also necessary to factor in the ever-capricious English weather.

The first step was to produce an accurate sketch of a kiwi profile so that a prototype could be drawn for the surveyor to use. Providing an exact sketch of a kiwi was always going to be a challenge. Many New Zealanders had never seen a kiwi let alone knew the proportions of its physical shape.

Above: Captain Harry Clark, 1919.
Left: Sergeant Major Percy
Blenkarne, 1918.
Below: Sergeant Major Victor Low
(circled), 5th Tunnelling Company,
1917.

It fell to Sergeant Major Percy Blenkarne from the Army Education Unit to provide a precise outline for the field survey team to use.

Blenkarne was not an artist as such but he certainly had a flair for drawing and was attached to the Education Unit as a drawing instructor. Prior to enlisting in the New Zealand Expeditionary Force, Blenkarne, a married man with one child, was a picture operator at the Globe theatre in Auckland. He arrived in Britain in August 1918 as part of the 39th reinforcement. It is not known if Blenkarne volunteered for the job of sketching the kiwi or was ordered to carry it out, but no doubt the prospect of a trip to the British Natural History Museum in London to find a true specimen was a great incentive to be involved in the project.[6]

It is difficult to determine whether he sketched the kiwi from a book of birds housed in the British Natural History Museum or from a mounted kiwi, or a combination of both. Both were part of the museum collections in 1919. Percy Blenkarne's kiwi sprouts the starchy whiskers detailed in the illustration by J G Keulmans in Buller's *A History of the Birds of New Zealand* (see page 91).

Blenkarne returned to Sling Camp with his outline drawing essential for the next stage in the process.

The second person involved with the design and construction of the kiwi was Sergeant Major Victor Low. It is not known when Percy Blenkarne and Victor Low joined forces on the project but they would have needed to have worked together to take the sketches to the next stage of redesigning the drawing to fit the kiwi onto Beacon Hill.

Sergeant Major Victor Low, who carried out the work of surveying the site for the kiwi, had served in Arras in France with the 5th Tunnelling Company. He was the third son of Matilda and Joseph Lo Keong (anglicised to Low), considered to be the first Chinese family in New Zealand.[7] Victor, who lived in Dunedin, joined up in January 1917 and was posted overseas late April 1917.

Victor Low had attended Canterbury College in Christchurch, New Zealand to undertake an engineering degree. There are no records to say that Victor completed his degree while living in New Zealand. However, given that he had completed a number of years studying engineering it is highly likely he would have had the necessary skills to work as a surveyor on the kiwi project. During his war experience in France in the Arras tunnels, as part of the New Zealand Engineer's Tunnelling Company, he had done exactly that type of task.

At the end of the war, when the New Zealand Tunnelling Company was repatriated to New Zealand as a unit, Victor Low had stayed on in Britain and become part of the education staff at Sling Camp. It is therefore feasible that he and Percy Blenkarne worked together as colleagues to get the image of the kiwi into a form that could be successfully used on Beacon Hill.

There were a number of technical challenges for the duo to resolve. As there was a gentle slope of about ten degrees above horizontal on Beacon Hill, Blenkarne's drawing of the kiwi had to be transposed on to the hill in such a manner that it would still retain its proper perspective when viewed from a distance. As the kiwi would not sit neatly on Beacon Hill as a flat cut-out image, Blenkarne's drawing had to be manipulated to fit the site.

The difficulty of working on the Beacon Hill site was elaborated on by Harry Clark in a letter to the *Marlborough Express* dated 26 September 1919. Clark stated,

The designing was made considerably more difficult owing to the various slopes of the hill, there being no one plain slope of even grade sufficiently large for the design. Owing to receding higher slopes it was necessary to distort the outline in order to obtain the proper perspective from the cross roads at the centre of the camp.[8]

Many discussions would have been held between the men as to where the best viewing location was within Sling Camp. Due to the parallax effects the Kiwi emblem would become distorted if viewed from a closer vantage point or a more distant one, so the choice of a viewing location was important.

It was decided that the kiwi should be a large emblem in line with other

APTERYX MANTELLI.

The Kiwi, Apteryx mantelli, *illustrated by J G Kuelmans from Buller's* A History of the Birds of New Zealand. © *The Trustees of the Natural History Museum, London.*

Percy Blenkarne's drawing of the proposed kiwi to go on Beacon Hill above Sling Camp, 1919.

YMCA Corner, looking up Gaza road towards the Kiwi on Beacon Hill 1919.

images carved into the chalk hills around Southern England, and be able to be viewed from a number of vantage points. The position selected to set out the actual kiwi site on Beacon Hill was from 'YMCA Corner' in Sling Camp close by the existing Tidworth-Gaza roads junction. Victor Low may have also used the main parade ground for Sling Camp (also near to the main Tidworth Road and a few metres from YMCA corner). The surveying observation point had an unobstructed view of Beacon Hill some 800 metres away.

YMCA corner was at the social heart of the camp. Tom Davidson, a young Otago soldier who later admitted that he was more interested in how he could manage to enjoy his incarceration in the camp by avoiding the hard work of scraping an emblem out of the chalk hillside and dodge education courses, noted the surveyor and assistants hard at work on YMCA corner. As a 93-year-old, in a letter to the Returned and Services Association (RSA) penned in 1992, he recalled that time in his life in Sling Camp. Tom Davidson commented, 'We were paraded

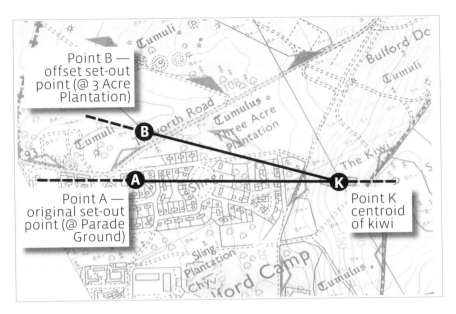

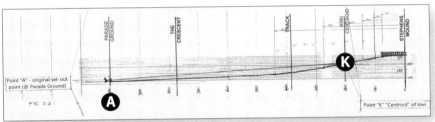

Top: A 1922 map of Sling Camp showing the sight line from YMCA Corner and the parade ground (A) to the site of the Bulford Kiwi (K).

Above: A sectional elevation created in 2015 showing the sightline north from YMCA Corner and the parade ground (A) towards Beacon Hill (K).

and marched to work on it (the kiwi) every morning. I saw the officer in charge of the survey party at work outside the YMCA hut getting the proportions right from this spot.'[9]

It is possible that the surveyors also used the major parade ground just to the right of YMCA corner where the flagpole was sited at the front of Sling Camp to carry out their work. This possibly arises because

The main parade ground at Sling Camp, 1919.

a well-publicised photo used by the Kiwi Polish Company was taken from a location from within the parade ground that is somewhat off-set from the flagpole, which was known to be near the Gaza Road frontage.

It would have been difficult to carry out any physical work on the kiwi until the weather cleared up. Right through the early spring months of 1919 Blenkarne and Low would have worked on creating the optical illusion required to project the correctly proportioned image. Up on Beacon Hill, the shape of the kiwi looks like a stretched out bird, quite distorted in its figure and form. But from 800 metres away the human eye is able to project a virtual image back onto the horizon and view the kiwi image true to its desired form, with a magnification factor on the horizontal dimension of around 125 percent.

How did they achieve this?

Victor Low's experience working in the Arras tunnels and surrounding area would have been priceless and a critical factor in the success of the project. His skill in using a theodolite to survey Beacon Hill was most likely coupled with a communication system of field telephones that would have allowed the various people involved —

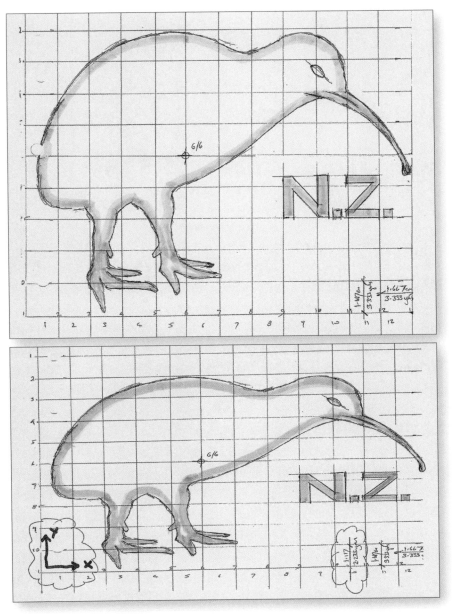

A copy of Blenkarne's original drawing of the kiwi (top) and (above) Blenkarne's kiwi scaled by 67 percent vertically to fit on Beacon Hill, 2015.

some on the hill and others in the parade ground — to communicate with each other effectively.

Victor Low would have already determined the intended size of the Bulford Kiwi before he started the project. Blenkarne's original drawing of the kiwi now proportionally adjusted to fit on Beacon Hill had been overlaid with a grid to enable the outline of the bird to be set out on the sloping contour of the site. A mid-point for the emblem would likely have been established first, taking into consideration the height and width available as determined by the topography of the hill. The most likely scenario the team would have followed would be to work out the shape of the perimeter of the emblem first, driving pegs into the ground at each significant marker.

As each peg was driven in, it would have been tagged with an identifying marker detailing its reference back to coded intersection points on the Blenkarne drawing. Once applied on the ten-degree slope, the squares became rectangles with a length to width ratio of about five to one. Thus the shape of the kiwi image on the hill became distorted when viewed 'bird's eye' from above but looked 'just right' when viewed horizontally from the parade ground some 800 metres away.

Once those rectangle reference points were pegged, it is likely that tapes were run between each one linking the whole outline of the bird. Once the outline of the kiwi had been marked out on the ground it was time to get the troops up the hill to carry out the excavation. That job fell to Captain Harry Clark, the third person in the trio to work on getting the kiwi onto Beacon Hill.

Captain Harry Clark, a mining engineer, had served in the NZEF right from the start of the war, enlisting in 1914 and serving at Gallipoli. He kept a diary throughout the war, recording and reflecting on his experiences. After recovering from wounds received at Gallipoli, he then went on to France and worked on maintaining the trenches while commanding a group of sappers. On 7 July 1916, in his words he 'met his Waterloo'.[10] Essentially Clark was sent up to the front line to maintain collapsed trenches and was with a working party when a

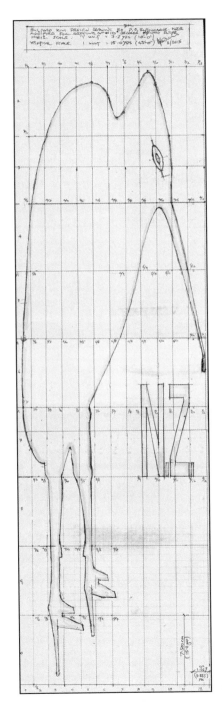

Bird's eye view of Blenkarne's kiwi 1919.

shell exploded in front of him knocking him out. This happened again, then he was dragged into a dugout by two soldiers before their ditch was bombed and they were all buried alive. Clark was dug out unconscious, hospitalised and suffered an extreme form of shellshock. He was passed unfit for further active service and repatriated to New Zealand. Clark recovered, and re-enlisted in October 1917. When he arrived in England in November 1918 he was sent to Sling Camp for administration work.

In November 1918 Harry Clark was appointed barracks and works officer at the camp, overseeing all building and maintenance work. He was expected to help keep the 'A' grade men busy with whatever construction work he could find around the camp. Men were put to work filling in training trenches and constructing a pigsty. After the March 1919 riots, Clark was required to utilise his engineering and management expertise to supervise New Zealand soldiers carrying out the repairs to the riot damage on buildings around the camp.

There they were — a triumvirate of skilled soldiers who found themselves grouped together and tasked with creating the largest kiwi image the world had ever seen as an emblem of the New Zealanders' wartime occupation of Sling Camp.

It is not certain as to when the actual digging of the Bulford Kiwi started. Harry Clark's diary states that he was only brought into the kiwi project after he and his team had completed all the repair work to the buildings damaged in the riots, which would have been well into April 1919 taking into consideration the extent of the damages and the adverse weather conditions.

Given that Clark had the responsibility for organising the men to do the necessary digging out of the emblem and the hauling of the dirt off site, this task would not have been undertaken while the ground was still frozen, especially in view of the recent riot. The weather proved to be a challenge right through the early spring months.

There are a number of newspaper accounts that detail how the Bulford Kiwi was made. While Clark recorded the basic information about the giant emblem and its final dimensions in his war diary, he did not keep a running record of how it was created, although he did write a letter to his parents about the construction of the giant bird and sent reports to New Zealand newspapers on its completion.

In his letter (undated) to his parents, Clark said he was enclosing a few 'snaps' of the completed kiwi emblem and that he had supervised the work. He wrote that he had been assisted by two sergeant majors, a surveyor and a draftsman, which would have been a reference to Victor Low and Percy Blenkarne.[11]

The area enclosed by the Bulford Kiwi was 21,260 square yards (17,776 square metres), and the newspaper reports sent by Harry Clark indicate that the troops excavated down to a depth of around one foot (0.3 metres) to expose the chalk. In his letter to the *Marlborough Express*, Clark stated that the emblem was 'cut out of the solid chalk and stands out in sharp contrast from the surrounding green of the hillside.'[12] It is not known what implements were used to carry the waste off site, possibly baskets or sacks of some description. Even with clear weather and the ability to recruit enough men to do the job it would have taken at least a month to six weeks of constant digging to remove the turf cover, hollow out the shape of the kiwi, and expose and lay bare the underlying white chalk.

Achieving the permanent visual impact of the emblem as originally intended was a demanding and exacting task. The physical construction required considerable human resources, careful direction of the men undertaking the digging and the effective management and supervision of the troops supplying the labour. Any errors in over-cutting the perimeter edge (even if made good) would be sensitive to future erosion damage and, while not noticeable close up on the actual slopes, would be obvious to the observer on the parade ground some 800 metres away.

Captain Harry Clark recorded the challenges he faced in a memo to senior officers written on 12 June 1919 in which he outlined three areas of concern that were impeding the completion of the kiwi. He appealed to senior officers for help to get the project back on track and completed in a timely manner.[13]

Clark's first complaint was that men, particularly those from the Wellington detachment, were not turning up for work. He noted that he had asked for 400 men each day but appeared to be agreeable to 250 men each day to work on Beacon Hill cutting out the kiwi. He logged the attendance of the various detachments. On Tuesday 10 June 1919, only fifteen of the Wellington men reported for duty. On 12 June, only forty-seven Wellington men turned up to dig the chalky soil and cart it to waste. By contrast Canterbury and Otago detachments had each provided 175 men every second day, which was still short of the manpower required to complete the job. The second point made was that the NCOs provided were not contributing to the day's work in the manner required, and they needed to be told to give more assistance in keeping the men at their task. Lastly, Clark objected to the fact that despite the reporting time being 9 a.m., only Canterbury men were complying with the order, and the other detachments were trickling in at 9.30 a.m.

Harry Clark's memo outlined several solutions to the problems. He wanted a stricter timetable enforced. He asked that all NCOs be directed to provide support for those in charge at the cutting front. Lastly, he wanted clearer communication lines as to where any manpower shortages might lie recorded by 4 p.m. on the preceding day that any particular detachment was required to work on the kiwi so he could manage the impacts of any shortfall.

It was obvious that as the soldiers started to be shipped home more efficiently there was a progressive disintegration in any enthusiasm that may have previously existed for the task. According to Harry Clark, officers, NCOs and 250 soldiers per day minimum were required up on the hill to dig, cart and dump the topsoil five-and-a half days a week in order for the kiwi to be completed in the allotted time.

Clark was successful in his petition. On 14 June 1919, an order from Brigadier-General Young's office was issued to the Canterbury, Otago and Wellington detachments, instructing them to provide 250 men on a daily basis with four NCOs supervising the work. The three

The completed Kiwi symbol on Beacon Hill June 1919.

units were also required to notify Sling Camp Headquarters in writing the day before whether or not they could contribute their full quota. A weekly schedule had been produced, rotating the three separate units with a reporting time for 'being ready to start work' of no later than 0900 hours.

And so, after all this effort, on 28 June 1919, the giant kiwi was finally completed. Symbolically this was the same day that peace was signed between Germany and the principal Allied Powers participating in WWI.

Captain Harry Clark celebrated the completion by sending a letter

Harry Clark with the Bulford Kiwi in the background, Sling Camp, 1919.

and photograph of the kiwi to New Zealand. The contents of that letter were distributed to newspapers across the country. In his letter, Clark noted, 'This emblem should last for hundreds of years and will in time be an historic landmark just like the "white horses". Nearly all the returned men will have passed through Sling Camp and I am sure that they will be glad to know that we have left our mark behind us.'[14]

Clark added, 'When on the morning that Peace was signed, the Kiwi was at last completed, the 'Diggers' who had toiled and sweated in the summer sun surveyed the result of their labours with pride and satisfaction.' He added that the dimensions of the kiwi covered an area

KIWI Emblem cut out of Chalk by the N.Z. Forces to commemorate their occupation of Sling Camp, Bulford, during the Great War. The Body covers an area of 1¼ acres, Height 420 ft., length of Bill 150 ft. Height of letters N.Z. 65 ft. Total area enclosed 4½ acres. The Emblem has been registered as a Military Encroachment by the Imperial Authorities and on behalf of the N.Z. Forces, its maintenance has been undertaken by the KIWI POLISH CO., Pty. Ltd., London.

The Chalk Kiwi – the official photograph used by The Kiwi Polish Company.

of one and a quarter acres (0.5 hectares), the height of it being 420 feet (128 metres), the length of the beak 150 feet (45.7 metres) and height of the letters N. Z. being 65 feet (19.8 metres).[15]

His final words about the kiwi, recorded both in his diary and in the letter home were that 'with a little attention from time to time the emblem should last for all time'. [16]

Two more actions were required by the New Zealand Expeditionary Force before it left for home. They needed to protect the kiwi emblem from animals and make sure it had regular maintenance. Someone in the New Zealand Army decided that it would be a good idea to approach the Kiwi Polish Company to see if they were interested in maintaining the emblem after the New Zealand contingent left for home and the camp was closed. It fell to Harry Clark to negotiate with the company as to how this could be arranged.

The Kiwi Polish Company, with a factory in Fulham, London, was a well-known product to many soldiers as its boot polish was purchased in large quantities by both the British and American armies in WWI. It was an Australian company, and the owner of the organisation used the name 'Kiwi' as a marketing strategy in recognition of his New Zealand wife Annie's heritage.

Correspondence between Clark and James Ramsay, the CEO of the Kiwi Polish Company, indicates that a deal was struck whereby the company would cover the cost of tending to the emblem and in return they would use the kiwi as a marketing tool for their product as the caretakers 'on behalf, and at the request of the New Zealand Forces'.[17]

Before the caretaking arrangement could be finalised, permission from the British Army for access to the site had to be gained. On 6 September 1919, the 'A' Group Commanding Officer at Sling Camp wrote to the British Southern Command requesting that the Kiwi Polish Company be granted a permanent permit of right of entry onto the site, which was controlled by the British Army.[18]

Southern Command advised that 'permission to the Kiwi Polish Company to maintain the Kiwi will be registered as a military encroachment by C.R.E [Commander Royal Engineers] Salisbury Plan, Bulford.' The engineers advised that a fence to stop sheep from damaging the excavated area would be an appropriate step to take in order for the emblem to survive.[19] encroachment form was forwarded by the Royal Engineers to the 'A' Group commander at Sling Camp which was passed on to the Kiwi Polish Company. The company duly signed the encroachment form and returned it in a letter agreeing to pay for the erection of a fence around the emblem and to care for the kiwi, and assuring the New Zealand Army that 'it will be our utmost endeavour to see that its design is in no way interfered with.'[20]

The last New Zealand soldiers marched out of Sling Camp on 1 November 1919 bound for home.[21] One of their last sights would have been of the giant kiwi they had carved out on Beacon Hill — an enduring reminder of the men who had trained at Sling Camp, those who had marched off to battle and didn't return, and those who had returned and dreamed of home.

On 5 November 1919 Captain Harry Clark handed Sling Camp back to the Royal Engineers of the Imperial Army.[22] With that action a brutal and unforgiving chapter of both New Zealand and Britain's history came to an end.

The sound of the men's boots on tarmac and hills might be gone, their voices and singing mere whispers on the wind, and, in time, the hutments they lived in would be demolished, but the kiwi remained indelibly imprinted onto Beacon Hill above Sling Camp — a guardian of those times and of those memories.

Part Two

— Chapter Eight —

The Kiwi Revisited: 1920–1950

There is something very sad about revisiting an old camp – alone. Boy did I feel lonely standing there. The place was full of memories and not a Digger in sight. I could hear the voices of cobbers, the sound of bugles, bands and bagpipes and the old penny-in-the-slot piano juke box that played incessantly every evening in the YMCA.[1]

EXCERPTS FROM GEORGE JENKINS LETTER, 1934

Not much is known about the Bulford Kiwi emblem in the early years after WWI. Certainly it was faithfully maintained by the Kiwi Polish Company. In 1923 the New Zealand Government asked the former Brigadier-General George Richardson to make enquiries in the United Kingdom as to whether the Kiwi was still being looked after by the Kiwi Polish Company, because no information had been received by the government about the success or otherwise of the arrangements made in 1919.

George Richardson wrote to Colonel Deedes of Southern Command in Salisbury on 16 January 1923, asking him for an update on the current state of the Kiwi emblem. It was obvious from Richardson's letter that former soldiers had been asking the government about the Kiwi and whether it was being well looked after.[2] Deedes replied on 17 March 1923, saying that he passed the emblem often, that it and the fence were in good condition and that he had recently seen men working on the chalk face of the Kiwi cleaning it up.

Photograph of the Bulford Kiwi taken by George Jenkins in 1934.

No doubt other former soldiers like George Jenkins returned over that post-war period to revisit the former Sling Camp training site that had been so significant in their lives during the war. George Jenkins noted the changes to the former camp on the back of the photograph he took of the Kiwi in 1934.

He wrote, 'The YMCA buildings stood on the area where the noticeboard is. The telephone poles were not there in WWI days. Not many of the hutments appear to be left here at the time this photo was taken in 1934.'[3]

When Jenkins visited the former camp site he sketched Sling Camp based on his memories from his times there in 1917 and 1918. He marked on the sketch where the practice areas for the bombing pit had been and the gas chamber where they had trained for possible gas attacks as part of their trench warfare instruction. He also recalled how they had 'toiled and sweated' while carrying out the exercises designed to ready them for what was to come at the front.

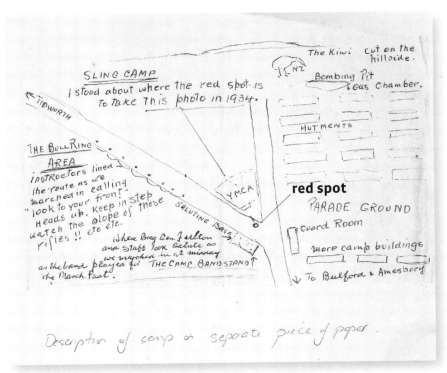

Sketch of Sling Camp and environs by George Jenkins 1934.

As Jenkins observed on his 1934 visit, as Sling Camp was absorbed into British military ownership the hutments he referred to were moved or demolished. Although the streets for the most part retained their wartime names, over time the area was turned into living quarters for military personnel based in various parts of the wider Salisbury Plain military zone.

The High Commissioner for London, Mr William Jordan, and his wife paid a visit to the area in 1938, visiting the Tidworth Military Cemetery, the former Sling Camp area and the Bulford Kiwi. Like George Jenkins, the High Commissioner would have noted the changes to the area since he had been a raw recruit at the camp in January 1918. The newspaper article recording the High Commissioner's visit to the area stated that the Kiwi emblem was 'maintained by the military authorities'.[4]

Indeed Sling Camp had changed in the intervening years as the British Army consolidated its holdings on Salisbury Plain. By the late 1930s the area looked remarkably different from the way it appeared in 1919.

At the outbreak of war in 1939 the British Government had to think again about the blazing white Kiwi emblem on Salisbury Plain as the threat of bombing raids became a reality. During peacetime the giant bird had been used as an unofficial landmark by commercial aircraft when flying from the continent to Britain, and at the start of the war it was quickly realised that the Luftwaffe was using it for the same purpose during bombing raids. In 1939 the Kiwi was covered up with clods of earth for the duration of the war. It must have worked as there are only 'three bomb holes at the top of Beacon Hill'.[5]

There is conflicting information about what happened to the Kiwi at the end of WWII. In New Zealand, the *Evening Post* reported in August 1945 that the district commander, a Major General Laurie, gave permission for the memorial to be restored and that the men of the Devonshire Regiment cut the growth and cleaned the Kiwi up.[6] The *Auckland Star* and *New Zealand Herald* newspapers both drew on the same information, generated from an unnamed London source, stating that the Kiwi was overgrown to such an extent that its outline had to be re-cut.[7] It is difficult to verify this report as the only Major General Laurie listed in the British Army retired from military service in 1943, and his only involvement with anything military in 1945 was with the Wiltshire Army Cadet Force. It also appears that the Devonshire Regiment was not in the vicinity in 1945. The Devonshire regiment in 1945 was posted to Burma, Singapore and Germany but were not based in the Tidworth area at that time.[8]

Another widely held and more accepted view as to how the Kiwi re-emerged from its war-time concealment is that the First Bulford Scout Group, established in 1908, cleaned up the Kiwi in 1948. Information from the First Bulford Scout Group's historic records state that the Kiwi stayed covered until 1948 when the Scout group

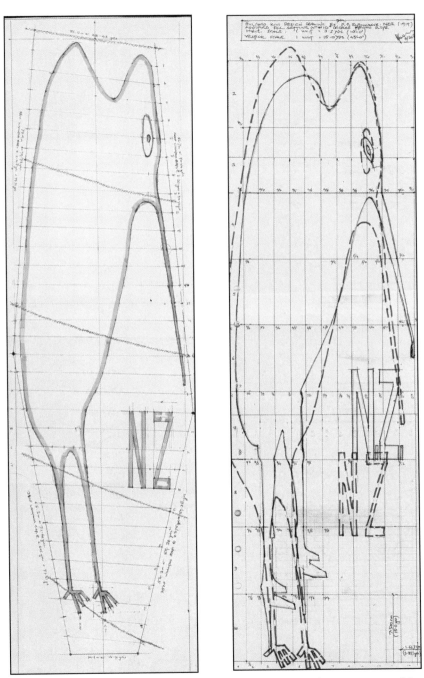

Bulford Kiwi drawings, 2015. Above left: The Kiwi in 1948. Above right: A comparison of the outline of the Kiwi in 1948 (solid line) and the original outline in 1919 (dashed line).

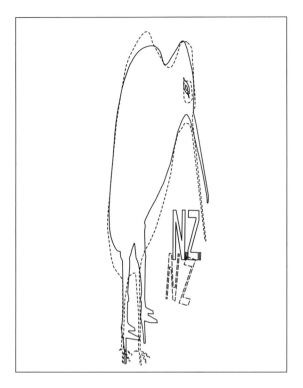

Digital scan of the Bulford Kiwi (2016) comparing the 1919 (solid line) and 1940s (dashed line) outlines.[9]

decided to uncover it nine years after it had been covered by earth. As their documentation explains:

> *This was no small task as the grass had taken root and the whole project had to be started from scratch just as the New Zealand soldiers had done all those years early (sic). The work was undertaken to remove the grass sods and cover the shape in clean chalk; the pit at the bottom of the hill is where they dug the chalk. They only had wheelbarrows, spades and ropes. It was very hard work and took a long time. Scouts and Cub Scouts (who were called Boy Scouts and Wolf Cubs) had to work very hard.*[10]

The task of clearing the Kiwi took many weeks, and after the project was completed the Chief Scout Lord Rowallen and the High Commissioner for New Zealand visited the scouts to see what they had accomplished. It is said that Lord Rowallen was so impressed with their efforts that he decided the name of the group should change to the '1st Bulford (Kiwi) Scout Group' and that the scouts should wear a kiwi on the point of their scarf. The scout group's information leaflet stated: 'This is the only Group in the world to have a Chief Scout change the name of the Group and instruct them to wear a badge in recognition of what they had done.'[11]

Regardless of whether it was the Devonshire Regiment or the First Bulford Scout Group that restored the Kiwi after the Second World War, the outline that emerged was somewhat different from the one that the New Zealand soldiers had left behind in 1919.

It is not surprising that the Kiwi's shape changed, considering that the drawing that guided the decision-making process by the New Zealand trio in 1919 was back in New Zealand. It had been taken home by Sergeant Major Percy Blenkarne and kept in his family for many years.

It seems that at this stage the Kiwi was adopted by the scouts as a project, and the caretaker employed by the Kiwi Polish Company, who had cared for the Kiwi after WWI, re-emerged to take up his duties again. That arrangement might have continued, but for the intervention of former Sergeant Major Percy Blenkarne.

‑ Chapter Nine ‑

Saving the Kiwi: 1950–1971

The position as we see it now is that everyone apparently wants to see the emblem maintained but no one wants to foot the bill.[1]

T M RAMSAY, JOINT MANAGING DIRECTOR KIWI POLISH COMPANY

The re-cut Kiwi slumbered on Beacon Hill during the late 1940s, somewhat isolated as the military landscape changed, tended intermittently by the Kiwi Polish Company retainer, the military and the local scout group. This state of partial obscurity of the emblem may have continued for many more years if, in 1950, Percy Blenkarne hadn't retraced his steps back to the former Sling Camp.

Blenkarne, who had sketched the diagram of the Kiwi in 1919 and who was on a long-term visit to Britain, had contacted the Kiwi Polish Company about the maintenance of the giant bird. After he received a reply from the company, Percy Blenkarne contacted the New Zealand London High Commissioner, William Jordan, to see if he could persuade him to support his idea of getting the New Zealand Government to take a closer interest in and involvement with the preservation of the emblem. Percy had done his homework and was prepared to advocate strongly for the Kiwi to be cared for by New Zealand interests. He was successful in getting the High Commissioner on his side.

The first inkling the New Zealand Government had that trouble was brewing over the care of the by-now historic Kiwi was when the High Commissioner wrote to the Minister of Defence, Thomas McDonald, on 6 July 1950 outlining a series of concerns that he felt the minister needed to be informed about.[2]

The first matter William Jordan raised was the question of the maintenance of the large emblem. Jordan explained that the 'enthusiast' – as he called the seventy-year-old caretaker – was paid £12 a year by the Kiwi Polish Company and had to buy his own weed killer. The tone of Jordan's letter suggested that he felt the caretaker was under paid for the rigour of the ongoing task. He suggested that the Kiwi Polish Company was losing interest in attending to the upkeep of the Kiwi. He reminded the minister of the Kiwi's history and that many New Zealand visitors went to Bulford expressly to visit it.

The High Commissioner enclosed a copy of the letter from the Kiwi Polish Company addressed to Percy Blenkarne, along with an official photograph of the Kiwi taken in 1919.[3] The letter revealed that the company extracted little if any advertising value from the association with the Kiwi emblem. It acknowledged that the company's commitment to maintaining the Kiwi was out of respect for, and as a memorial to, the men who were stationed at Sling Camp during WWI. The company also disclosed that they would be very interested to hear the outcome of Percy Blenkarne's discussion with the High Commissioner over the future maintenance of the Kiwi. The letter was signed by H Ramsay, Advertising Manager.

The conclusion William Jordan was drawing was that with an elderly caretaker, an apparently declining maintenance record and influenced by Percy Blenkarne's concerns, the High Commissioner felt that it was time for the New Zealand Government to consider paying for the maintenance of the emblem. William Jordan outlined a plan as to how a recommended £50 a year contribution by the New Zealand Government could be used to preserve this important national treasure.[4]

The High Commissioner cobbled together a list of people he suggested might help maintain the Kiwi, including a local British ex-serviceman group and the camp commander of the nearby British troops, who might provide an occasional fatigue party to care for the Kiwi. He asked for a financial commitment from the government before he proceeded to talk to any local people about what options they might support.[5]

The Minister of Defence, Thomas McDonald, a veteran of both world wars, acted swiftly and decisively on William Jordan's letter. He scrawled on a note attached to the photograph of the Kiwi sent to him by Jordan — 'It would be hard to resist this I think.'[6]

McDonald's support for New Zealand to take ownership of the Kiwi's maintenance came from the Returned and Services Association (RSA). Once the RSA had been informed of the facts surrounding the current state of the Kiwi emblem, they backed the minister's proposition and offered to share the cost of the Kiwi's upkeep with the government. The proposal achieved by the RSA and communicated by letter to McDonald on 16 October 1950 was that the association would add £20 to the government's contribution of £30 for the upkeep of the Kiwi.[7] McDonald acknowledged the co-payment and explained that the Army would administer the fund as part of its budget.[8]

It was an elegant solution to an ongoing problem.

The minister then approached his cabinet colleagues with a sewn-up deal. On 19 October 1950, a memorandum from the Minister of Defence's office was circulated to all cabinet members.[9] It outlined the basic history of the Kiwi and the current maintenance situation along with the financial arrangement with the RSA. Thomas McDonald concluded his memo with a recommendation to his fellow politicians:

It is a question now whether government should accept responsibility for the future maintenance of the emblem and in this connection I would recommend that the government make an annual contribution of £30 a year.[10]

Cabinet approved the recommendation on 24 October 1950.[11] The army, the secretary to treasury, and the controller and auditor general were all officially notified the following day.[12]

The minister had rescued the emblem. He had astutely saved money by splitting the financial obligation in creating a partnership with the powerful RSA and simultaneously he signalled to the country that the government was taking its responsibility for a national icon seriously, albeit an icon that was overseas.

In its November 1950 edition of the *RSA Review* an article about the Bulford Kiwi appeared quoting the defence minister as stating:

> *that up to the present the maintenance had been looked after by the Kiwi Polish Company who paid £12 a year to keep the Kiwi in good order and free of weeds. The company, however, is now losing interest, and the man who has looked after it for all these years is now 70 years of age.*[13]

The RSA article explained that the emblem was a permanent memorial to a First World War camp site and held sentimental memories for old soldiers from that era. The article concluded that the New Zealand High Commissioner to London had suggested that the maintenance of the emblem should be the responsibility of the New Zealand Government. The RSA article finished the report by stating in bold type that the NZRSA had informed the government that it would share the maintenance responsibility by offering £20 per year towards its upkeep.[14]

That appeared to be the end of the matter. The government and the RSA had saved the Kiwi.

However, on 9 November 1950, the RSA and the Minister of Defence each received letters from Mr T M Ramsay, the joint managing director of the Kiwi Polish Company, rebuking them for statements made in the published RSA article and bluntly refuting the idea that the company had 'lost interest' in maintaining the emblem.[15]

In a strongly worded letter to the *RSA Review* editor, Ramsay clarified the company's position. First, he set the record straight by pointing out that the idea that the company should even be involved in tending to the Kiwi had been opposed by some WWI veterans from the start as they felt it was a government responsibility. Ramsay added that the company had never suggested it give up its Kiwi maintenance programme. He reminded the editor that his company had paid for the upkeep of the Kiwi as a gesture of respect for the New Zealand troops from WWI, not for any commercial gain. Mr Ramsay explained that it was very difficult finding anyone who wanted to do gardening work of this nature and that they were very happy to continue with the current caretaker or any replacement person. The final paragraph of the letter stated that the writer felt the company had been treated unfairly, especially as the RSA newsletter was circulated widely amongst 'Kiwis' whom the company had 'claimed as friends for so many years'. With this thought in mind, Mr Ramsey reiterated that the company had 'never lost interest in this maintenance' and trusted that 'the impression will be quickly corrected'.[16]

The Minister of Defence received a copy of the Kiwi Polish Company letter sent to the RSA with an accompanying letter where Mr Ramsay pointed out that he trusted that the minister would take whatever steps he could to rectify the wrong impression created by his comments.[17]

It was a delicate situation. The New Zealand Government had been briefed by its High Commissioner to London as to the current status of the Kiwi. On the basis of that information and advice, the government and the RSA had finessed a solution that was beneficial to all concerned. Now the deal threatened to blow up in their collective faces.

Two official responses were made to Mr Ramsay's letter.

The first came from the Minister of Defence, Thomas McDonald, on 22 November 1950 to the managing director Mr Ramsay in Australia. The minister explained the series of events that led the New Zealand Government to conclude that the Kiwi Polish Company no longer wished to pay for the maintenance of the Kiwi site. He explained that the letter sent by Mr H Ramsay, the advertising manager for the company, to Mr Percy Blenkarne, which was subsequently shared with the High Commissioner, was interpreted by all parties as the Kiwi Polish Company wishing to transfer the care of the Kiwi to another party. In fact the letter stated 'As mentioned during our conversation, the time has now come when the New Zealand authorities in London might on behalf of their Ex-Servicemen Associations, consider the maintenance of the emblem coming directly under their control.'[18]

The Minister of Defence explained the misunderstanding and stated that the government had been acting in good faith on the matter and regretted any upset it had caused. The minister's letter offered to withdraw the government's offer to fund the Kiwi should the company wish to continue to fund the emblem and on behalf of the government thanked the company for their efforts and expense in the upkeep of the Kiwi.[19]

The second letter was sent by the army secretary, F B Dwyer, to the manager of the Kiwi Polish Company in Auckland. It appears to be a courtesy letter to make sure the New Zealand end of the organisation was aware of the stance of the New Zealand Government on the matter.[20]

The RSA did publish an article in January 1951 praising the Kiwi Polish Company for its dedication to maintaining the Kiwi and noting the numerous difficulties in doing so, but did not actually address its earlier statement that the Kiwi Polish Company 'had lost interest' in maintaining the Kiwi.[21]

However, despite the RSA's fulsome tribute the damage had been done.

In an effort to avoid any further miscommunication the army secretary wrote to T M Ramsay asking what the company now wished to do. On 26 February 1951 T M Ramsay wrote to the army secretary concerning the Kiwi. In a forthright message he said, 'The position as we see it now is that everyone apparently wants to see the emblem maintained but no one wants to foot the bill.'[22]

Ramsay stated that the matter was now in the hands of the New Zealand Government. In his view the government had to decide whether to carry on with its planned upkeep of the Kiwi with the RSA or to look at other options. T M Ramsey proposed two other possibilities for the government to consider — hand it back to the Kiwi Polish Company for them to continue to maintain the Kiwi or do a three-way split between the RSA, the government and the Kiwi Polish Company. Ramsay was quite clear in his communication — you decide and let us know. He sent a copy of his letter to the secretary of the RSA.

On 13 March 1951 a memo was written for the Minister of Defence recommending that the New Zealand Government proceed with its plan to maintain the Kiwi jointly with the RSA.[23]

The minister wrote to T M Ramsay on 12 April 1951 informing him of the government's decision. He thanked the company for what it had done over the more than twenty-five years it had looked after the Kiwi. He stated that he regretted the misunderstanding that had occurred and reiterated that the New Zealand Government acknowledged that the work had been carried out by the company as a purely altruistic gesture of respect to the WWI soldiers. He concluded his letter with a firm declaration:

Therefore in relieving your Company of the responsibility for future maintenance, I am pleased to be able to say that this is being done not because your company wishes to be relieved of the work or expense involved, but because the Government is in a better position to find a solution to the labour problem presented.[24]

At this stage the New Zealand Government was confident that it had matters in hand. It had met its responsibilities when challenged by Percy Blenkarne to step up and look after its own unique WWI memorial. It had secured the backing of the influential RSA. It had been prudent in its financial commitments. It had resolved its differences with the Kiwi Polish Company. Now the London High Commission would work with the RSA to care for the Kiwi emblem.

What could possibly go wrong?

After the Kiwi's maintenance budget had been secured, the role of the High Commissioner to London, William Jordan, was to find the necessary person or organisation to care for the emblem. In July 1951 Jordan described the process he had followed in a letter to the Minister of Defence. Despite his earlier optimism that a British service organisation would be able to tend the Kiwi, he was turned down by the British Legion and turned to the commander at Bulford Camp for help.

His mission ended with an agreement being struck with the 1st Bulford (Kiwi) Scout Troop in the latter part of 1951. The troop was given a grant of £5.5s.0d a year to look after the Kiwi. Jordan ended his letter by saying, 'I think, therefore, you can rest assured that the Kiwi will be kept in good order from now on.'[25]

This was not to be.

Jordan retired from his position and returned to New Zealand. Whether the Kiwi was regularly maintained by the Scout troop is a moot point. But in 1953 Percy Blenkarne received a letter from a Mr Bonner who had cared for the Kiwi as an employee of the Kiwi Polish Company. He wanted Blenkarne to know that the emblem was covered in weeds and in a state of disrepair. Mr Bonner offered to take on the task of maintaining the Kiwi and restoring it to 'first-class order'.[26]

In December 1953 an unnamed person representing the New Zealand Government wrote a report on the state of the Kiwi. The unsigned report summarised the facts. The Kiwi was suffering from neglect. No one knew who the current scoutmaster of the 1st Bulford (Kiwi) troop was. It appeared that the clean-up was intermittent and that no one was in charge of any maintenance programme. The report reiterated that the Bonner family was available to recommence maintaining the Kiwi.[27]

Another report was written for the government on 2 April 1954 with the author, a senior liaison army officer attached to the London High Commission, reiterating that the Kiwi was in a distressed state and that Mr Bonner was willing to resume caretaker duties.[28]

The Bonner family were again engaged to look after the Kiwi by the New Zealand Government in January 1955 for £12 a year.[29]

There are few other archival references to the Kiwi at Sling Camp. In 1959 there was an exchange of correspondence between the New Zealand Army and the London High Commission about the increase in maintenance costs for the Kiwi. As from the beginning of that year the caretaker was receiving £20 a year, an increase of £8, which appeared to lack authorisation from the army. The High Commission, when challenged on the increase, replied that it was unaware the payment came from the army vote.

A response from the New Zealand Army on 25 July 2016 to an Official Information Act (OIA) request by the author stated, 'Officials interpreted Cabinet's approval for £30 annual expenditure on the Kiwi to be an upper spending limit. Actual annual expenditure appears more often than not to have been less than this amount.'[30]

If this was the case, then it doesn't explain the queries by army officials when the payment for the maintenance of the Kiwi crept up to £20 a year in 1959 nor that the London High Commission was unaware of who paid the Kiwi's maintenance bill. The OIA response to the author went on to state, 'The only surviving records that could be traced relating to expenditure on the Bulford Kiwi are held at Archives New Zealand in Wellington. Unfortunately those records do not appear to have been maintained beyond 1960.'[31]

The New Zealand file on the Kiwi was finally stamped 'closed' on 29 October 1971 without any additional information being added.

– Chapter Ten –

The Modern Day Kiwi: 1971 to the present day

I thought I was seeing things! There was thick mist on the lowland and over on Beacon Hill, there appeared to be a giant white Kiwi patrolling the hillside.
LIEUTENANT COLONEL DANNY MACKNESS, 2017[1]

Few records if any are kept about the Kiwi emblem in the 1970s. It appears that those parties formerly involved in its upkeep, namely the New Zealand Government, the caretaker and the local Bulford Kiwi Scout pack, simply lost interest.[2] In 1980 the weed-infested Kiwi suddenly burst into public awareness once again when its plight was brought to New Zealand's attention by *The Press*. The RSA and the New Zealand Government conducted a public spat over the Kiwi, but this time, unlike in the 1950s, they were on opposing sides.

This part of the Kiwi's history started early in 1980, well before the story hit any headlines. Earlier in the year a British Army officer, Colonel P W Herring, the garrison adjutant based in the Bulford and Tidworth Administration Unit in Bulford appealed to the New Zealand Government for support in an effort to save the Kiwi carving from extinction. Colonel Herring was reported as stating that in the past the New Zealand Government had partially financed local volunteers and the British Army to keep the bird maintained. However as that source of money had dried up he was looking to the

New Zealand Government for a financial contribution and no doubt for some leadership on the issue.[3]

The RSA had been aware of the request for some months. Behind the scenes they swung into political action, writing to the London High Commissioner, Les Gandar, in May 1980 and contacting members of the New Zealand parliament asking for support. In addition, the RSA alerted its members in its August 1980 *Review* publication to the worsening state of the giant bird and that the British Army was seeking funds to restore it.[4]

On 2 September 1980, the Member of Parliament for Papanui, Mike Moore, lodged a written question to the Minister of Defence, David Thomson, as to whether he had seen the RSA article and, if so, what was the government doing about restoring the WWI symbol. Seven days later the minister responded in parliament. He explained that this emblem was one of many WWI New Zealand 'reminders' in the United Kingdom that were 'increasingly becoming casualties to the ravages of time and the elements'. The minister's response indicated that the government funding had stopped in 1967 and that the emblem had now 'deteriorated beyond recognition'. The minister stated that the government could not justify the funds to restore and maintain the war memorial into the future.[5]

A few days later, on 17 September 1980, the full story appeared in the Christchurch *Press* when the newspaper accused the government of 'turning its back' on the historic war memorial.[6] The article detailed the deteriorating state of the sixty-one-year-old emblem and the bid by the British Army to save the Kiwi from what seemed certain demise. The government was reported as 'refusing to spend a cent' on the historic emblem despite it being referred to as an 'impressive work' and linked to prehistoric chalk figures located nearby. The article added, in a private comment made to the reporter, that 'if New Zealand could afford to send the Prime Minister's social secretary to India and China with him, then perhaps it could afford to restore the giant chalk Kiwi of Bulford.'[7]

In that same newspaper report the RSA made a blunt statement refuting the government's position by noting that a mere $1,000 would have made a significant contribution to the emblem's restoration.

The government was forced into publicly stating their position that, 'the expense and effort to restore it, and then to continue to maintain it, is such that the Government could not justifiably make funds available'.[8]

At this point New Zealand formally forfeited all rights to and responsibilities for the iconic Kiwi emblem. Once the ministerial statement was published, it seemed like the end of an era. The commitment the government had made in 1950 was null and void.

Here was the problem. The British Army wanted the Kiwi, sitting in the backyard of one of its largest military bases, restored. It asked the New Zealand Government for financial assistance. In the circumstances it wasn't an unreasonable request. The Australian Government contributed funds to the upkeep of their two Australian insignia at the nearby Fovant Badge WWI memorial so why couldn't the New Zealand Government do likewise? However the New Zealand Government was unmoved and stood fast on its refusal to help. The RSA wanted to see the iconic Kiwi restored and preserved, but just as thirty years previously no one wanted to pay.

Reflecting on that period some thirty-seven years later in a personal interview, the Honourable Mike Moore commented, 'I recall my involvement with a bit of regret that I never followed it up.' He added, 'The nation is measured by what it remembers and if it doesn't remember it, it will repeat it.'[9]

At the same time as that debate was occurring in New Zealand in 1980, a major in command of a squadron of British soldiers assigned to NATO, unaware of both the financial request from his own army and the hot debate and friction between various parties in New Zealand, entered the scene and took matters into his own hands.

Major (later Lieutenant Colonel) Danny Fisher, the officer commanding 249 Signal Squadron AMF (L)[10] had just brought his men back from a NATO operation in the Arctic Circle. Typically this squadron was based in Norway during the winter period of operations and in Turkey for the summer deployment. As a NATO force, 249 Signal Squadron answered to an American commanding officer operating out of Europe and, although based in Britain, did not report to any British chain of command — only to NATO.[11]

Fisher and his men arrived at Bulford Camp, next to the former Sling Camp site, in the British summer of 1980. The squadron had some time on its hands before it departed for Turkey. Initially, Fisher responded to a request from an army friend to do some restoration work on the nearby WWI chalk Fovant Badges memorial. It was after that repair work had been completed, with their trucks and equipment readied for transportation to Istanbul and only a few days left before their deployment to Turkey, that the squadron set eyes on the dilapidated Kiwi.

As Fisher recalls, 'It was good fitness training to run up Beacon Hill right by the Kiwi. I lived nearby and used to take the dog up there. The Kiwi itself was totally overgrown and looked a real mess. There was no fence or anything. It was exposed to the elements and livestock.'[12]

Fisher asked his men to clean it up in a matter of a three days, in up to fourteen-hour shifts, before they left for their next mission. Their reward was a few beers and a couple of extra days off. It is important to note that 249 Signal Squadron was not ordered to do this task. Essentially the men did it for Danny Fisher. The fact that the squadron was not controlled from within the British Army structure meant that they had the freedom to undertake what they saw as an unusual one-off project in between missions.

And so the squadron, all 150 of them, minus the clerical staff, set their backs to the task. A number of comments from former soldiers from the squadron indicated that had they been ordered to do the job from within the army command itself they would have found a way to get out of it. They did it for their commanding officer in the first instance, a little begrudgingly initially, then with pride as they learned more about the historical significance of the Kiwi emblem and of the hardships faced by the New Zealand forces based in Sling Camp in 1919.[13]

Photograph of the restored Kiwi in 1980 taken from a vantage point close to where the Kiwi was surveyed in 1919.

As Stephen Fielding, a past member of 249 Signal Squadron, recalled:

It was hard back-breaking work, the weather strangely hot for Bulford because it always seemed to rain there most of the time. That first day, some were set to work weeding it, others re-cutting the outline of the emblem.

The next day it was finish off the cutting and then the real back-breaking work began, carrying sandbags up from the chalk pit at the bottom of the hill to the Kiwi where a team of men with rakes, shovels and forks spread the chalk across the surface. The body of the Kiwi was not as washed away as the legs were but were still about 1 to 2 feet lower than the correct level, so you can imagine how many sandbags were lifted to try and bring it back to life. On the Thursday it was decided by someone to try and help a little bit to bring some vehicles in from a nearby chalk quarry. It did help but also caused a slight problem because when this chalk was dropped onto the Kiwi compared to the chalk from the chalk pit at the base of the hill, this imported chalk had a pinkish tinge to it. This was quite quickly remedied by laying a very thin layer of chalk over the said area of pink chalk.[14]

Aerial photograph of the restored Buford Kiwi 1980. The men from the 249 Squadron are formed into the squadron numbers on the Kiwi.

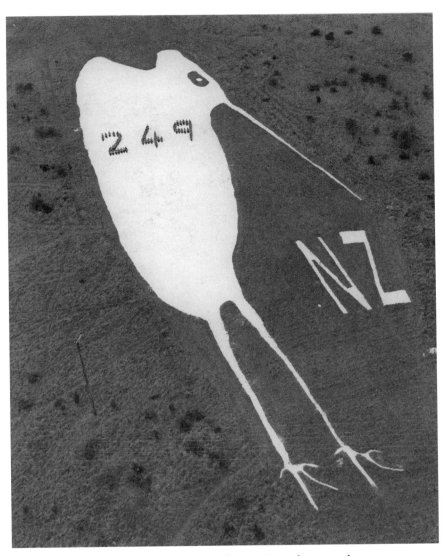

Photograph of the restored Kiwi 1980. The 249 Squadron numbers are configured on the body of the emblem.

Soldiers from 249 Squadron shovelling chalk onto the emblem, 1980.

Fisher's motivation for his actions was based on the decisive military quote from Admiral Grace Murray Hopper that he followed, 'It is often easier to ask for forgiveness than to ask for permission.'[15] As far as he was concerned it was a job that needed to be done and it was soldier to soldier. He wasn't going to go through a chain of command asking someone senior to him in Europe to authorise the clean-up. It was a job that required some effort, and he and his men had a short span of time in which to carry it out so he wasn't about to waste it on seeking permission. In Fisher's mind it was something the present-day soldiers could do for the soldiers from a previous era. The British Army was interested, however, and while cleaning up the Kiwi emblem Fisher was challenged by a garrison officer from the main Bulford and Tidworth Camp, who wanted to know what they were doing up on the site. Fisher's response was that it was a job that needed doing and his men were doing it. This was apparently accepted, and they were left alone to carry out the restoration task.[16]

As well as restoring the Kiwi, a year later, in 1981, Fisher set up the Kiwi

Trophy Challenge. Every member of 249 Signal Squadron participated in a gruelling cross-country run and marksmanship competition that started and finished at the site of the Kiwi emblem.

From 1980 onwards the duty of caring for and maintaining the Kiwi emblem was seen as a legacy task and part of the job carried out by all 249 Signal Squadron commanders and units. In 1986 Major (later Brigadier) Jonathan Cook, Officer Commanding 249 Signal Squadron, had a cairn built within the actual Kiwi enclosure with a commemorative plaque noting the history of the WWI emblem as he understood it. Once again, no permission from the army was sought. Cook said,

Having run the Kiwi Trophy in my first year in command (1985), I was in total ignorance of what it was all about and so did my rather sketchy research into the Kiwi and thought it would be good to put up something to explain why it was there. The NZ High Commission were not in any way involved with the idea to erect the cairn and plaque; neither were my chain of command — all too much hassle. I just did it and presented it as a fait accompli. It did make sense to me though to invite the New Zealand High Commissioner [Bryce Harland] to come and unveil it when we ran the Kiwi Trophy the following year (1986) and so he did just that and presented the Trophy prizes as well [on 11 July 1986].[17]

Colonel Paul Oldfield described it as part of the job description he inherited when he took up the position commanding the squadron in 1991. 'Looking after the Kiwi came with the job,' he said. Again the independence of 249 Signal Squadron was a strength that gave the soldiers the ability to carry out the unusual task of maintaining the memorial. Along with the upkeep of the Kiwi, 249 Signal Squadron kept up the annual tough challenge to win the highly coveted Kiwi trophy.[18]

It seemed that while 249 Signal Squadron was in existence the Kiwi was safe.

All that changed in 2003 when 249 Signal Squadron was disbanded. At that point the squadron's role in maintaining the emblem could well have been in jeopardy except for the fact that the majority of commanding officers of the new 3rd (United Kingdom) Division Signal Regiment were previous commanding officers of 249 Signal Squadron. It appears that the transition in care for the emblem has occurred seamlessly over the years with the merging of the 249 culture of looking after the Kiwi into the newly formed 3rd (United Kingdom) Division Signal Regiment. While the present-day soldiers' knowledge about the history of the emblem they maintain may be patchy, the on-going responsibilities associated with the giant bird remain embedded in their culture. The soldiers constantly refer to it as 'our Kiwi'.

Over the years the Kiwi has had a number of 'facelifts', with new chalk pieces being spread across its surface to brighten its form. A rabbit-proof fence has been added around its perimeter along with a permanent edging to protect its outline.

Today the Tidworth, Netheravon and Bulford Garrison has a commander responsible for overseeing the combined camps. The current commander, Colonel Steve Lawton, while acknowledging the particular historical connection between the Signals regiment and the Kiwi emblem, is quick to point out that the entire army based on Salisbury has a keen affection for and attachment to the historic emblem. He says that it is now part of the British Army culture.[19]

The army is proud of the tradition and heritage behind their guardianship of the bird and view their involvement as part of army tradition. Many a soldier who has been based at Bulford has a story to tell of their first encounter with the historic emblem and their curiosity as to how a flightless bird from half way around the world came to be cut out in the chalk hills above their base.

The deputy commander of the Garrison, Lieutenant Colonel Danny Mackness, said,

My first glimpse of the Kiwi was in 1983 when I was on an army exercise on Salisbury Plain Training Area. We arrived late at night, slept in the back of the trucks and when I woke up early the next morning and looked

Aerial photo of the Kiwi showing the clean-up operation taking place. Note the people clustered around the 'N', and the pile of grey stones on the Kiwi's back.

out of the back of the truck, I thought I was seeing things! There was thick mist on the lowland and over on Beacon Hill, there appeared to be a giant white Kiwi patrolling the hillside.[20]

The Kiwi on the hill has infiltrated many aspects of British Army life. The Garrison flag has a Kiwi as part of its insignia, and the local school bears the name 'The Bulford Kiwi School'; the military barracks adjacent to the Kiwi is called 'Kiwi Barracks'. The Kiwi has become more than just a part of the military landscape. Where once it was a bold white slash standing out starkly against the bare hill and seen for miles, now it appears more 'at home' in its surroundings. It is more mellow and softened into the landscape, obscured by trees and unable to be seen from the road as it used to be in 1919, yet its presence is there on Beacon Hill overlooking Salisbury Plain and part of the largest British Army base in the world.

Sling Camp and all the men who were based there have gone. Some of their letters, postcards, diaries and photographs telling of their time and experiences at Sling Camp still exist. Their stories have been told down through the generations, and rightly or wrongly the guardianship of their Kiwi emblem has been bequeathed by default to the British Army.

The future of the Kiwi now lies in the hands of the soldiers on Salisbury Plain.

Lieutenant Colonel Danny Fisher summed the story up, referring to it as 'the legacy passed down through the ages and between soldiers, not governments'. There is an enduring promise inherent in these words that reflect more than maintaining an emblem from a bygone age. It contains an intimate understanding between soldiers about sacrifice, duty and loss. As Fisher recently said to me, the emblem now embodies a legacy 'to the old soldiers in the new country from the young soldiers in the old country. Our link is carved forever in the timeless hills of Salisbury Plain.'[21]

Postscript

ON 12 JUNE 2017 HERITAGE ENGLAND FORMALLY LISTED THE KIWI EMBLEM AS A PROTECTED HISTORIC SITE.

The listing states, 'This monument is scheduled under the Ancient Monuments and Archaeological Areas Act 1979 as amended, as it appears to the Secretary of State to be of national importance.'[1]

And so, as Captain Harry Clark said back in September 1919, 'With a little attention from time to time the emblem should last for all time.'[2]

Harry Clark, c1917.

Major Danny Fisher, 1980.

Acknowledgements

The end result of writing a book like this reveals a vast cohort of extraordinary people, who have encouraged, pushed, criticised and cajoled me over the past four years. Without them and all those internet, email and text connections I would not have come this far.

I am indebted to Margaret Belton, the matriarch of the Fanselow, Belton, Hart and Clark families, who set me on my way with a quote from Goethe: 'The moment one commits oneself then providence also moves. Boldness has genius, power and magic.' Goethe, along with photographs of many of the soldiers whose lives have been shared in the book, has accompanied me at my place of work, day and night.

Thanks go to Dolores Ho, archivist at the Kippenberger Military Archive, National Army Museum, Waiouru. The National Army Museum was my first port of call on this quest and the treasures I discovered there were significant. It convinced me that ultimately I would find answers to my questions and that these riches must be shared with the nation.

Families are often the last to be acknowledged by writers but I want to thank my husband Barry Brown upfront. He is my sternest critic and my most ardent supporter. He has lived the book with me; clambered all over the magnificent Kiwi emblem, tape in hand on the chilliest of English summer days; listened to my 3 a.m. thoughts and questions and read every chapter, red pen in hand. Your encouragement and faith in me has been inspiring.

I want to thank Tracey Borgfeldt from Bateman Publishing who has calmly talked me through all aspects of the book right from my first visit, giving me the confidence that ultimately it would be published.

New Zealand is blessed that within a small precinct in Wellington lies the National Library, National Archives and, until a recent earthquake, the Ministry of Defence Library. All of these institutions have become very familiar to me over the years, as have the contents of their respective cafes. I acknowledge the expertise, dedication and professionalism of those staffs which has always been readily shared with no question being too challenging to answer. In particular I want to record my deep appreciation to Linda McGregor, senior research librarian at the Alexander Turnbull Library, who has helped me problem-solve my way through the maze of questions and challenges to track down family members who were possible sources of information for the book. Some of those challenges were formidable but we persevered and for the most part we were successful.

I would like to thank the staffs in all those archives and libraries for giving me permission to use their material in the book.

Librarians and museum curators from modest to large institutions across the country have been contacted for the merest snippet of information. All of them have replied with alacrity; some have been able to use their local knowledge to track down elusive sources for the book. These important repositories of our past are a marvel, and the people who staff them are welcoming, dedicated and hardworking.

Families of the people in my story have provided me and, subsequently, the book with a richness of cherished personal material that I have been able to weave into this story about our nation's past. Those long-treasured records have breathed life and insight into the story and given families an opportunity to revisit their own past and appreciate how their own personal histories have added to our nation's narrative. My gratitude goes to the Hart, Belton and Clark families, Nancie Allison and the Stewart family, the Lloyd family, the Young family, Noni Kenny, Mrs Blenkarne, David Hamblin, and Mike and Annette Batchelor.

I want to make special mention of Jane Tolerton, who has always been a phone call or email away. You have been an important sounding board and traveller with me.

I have had an eclectic group of people who have provided me with advice and encouragement as I wrote the book. Thank you Chris Pugsley, Sue Baker-Wilson, my editors at large, Sue Gates and Len Marr.

Early on in my writing, Sean Brosnahan, the curator of Toitu Otago Settlers Museum, encouraged me to connect with the very active Chinese community in Dunedin. I am grateful for the support I have received from both Sean and that community along with the opportunity to share the information about the huge contribution made by Victor Low (Lo Keong) to the creation of this most New Zealand of icons. My thanks go to Dr Jim Ng and Malcolm Wong for their interest in the book.

Richard Hemi, professional practice fellow and lecturer at the University of Otago school of Surveying, has helped decipher the technical digital data gleaned from scanning the current Kiwi on Beacon Hill and comparing its outline with the original 1919 carving. Richard's professional interest and enthusiasm has helped provide concrete evidence to underpin or demolish the various hunches and assumptions I and others have made about the Kiwi seen on Beacon Hill today. Along with Richard's expertise I have used the services of Peter James-Stephen from BDS Calne Ltd UK, who carried out the digital survey of the Kiwi site. Mike Wingfield helped co-ordinate many of the arrangements behind the scenes for the digital scanning process; he was a technical sounding board and accompanied us on our scramble over the Kiwi.

Special thanks go to the men and women from the British Army. In particular I would like to acknowledge Lieutenant Colonel Danny Mackness, Lieutenant Colonel Danny Fisher, Brigadier Jonathan Cook and the soldiers of 249 Signal Squadron, colloquially referred to as the 'Arctic Warriors', for their dedication to the upkeep of the Kiwi from 1980 to 2003, when the 3rd Division Signal Regiment assumed that responsibility. There is no doubt in my mind that had it not been for the intervention in 1980 of Danny Fisher and his men, the Kiwi would be a faint memory of a relic from WWI. Danny and Jonathan have been companions for the latter part of the book, spurring me on with encouraging words fortified by a military 'can do' attitude. I have been so impressed by the passion, pride and love for the Kiwi that the British Army holds. It floats regally on the flag mast at Tidworth Camp

Garrison Headquarters and is the focus for the rigours of training for the annual Kiwi Challenge held on the slopes of Beacon Hill. To all intents and purposes it is the British Army's Kiwi now.

Along with my helpers in New Zealand I have had a stunning array of supporters in Britain. Foremost of those is Rosemary Meeke, the editor of *Drumbeat*, the monthly newsletter of the Tidworth, Netheravon and Bulford Garrison Community on Salisbury Plain. Rosemary has answered every query I have tossed her way and provided personal support on my two trips to the area. The contemporary stories about the Kiwi have been well chronicled under her stewardship as editor. I have many friends in the UK who have hosted me on my trips, provided me with a bed and encouragement, acted as chauffeurs and plied me with many cups of tea and cake over the years I have been researching material for this book.

My special thanks go to the Chinese Poll Tax Heritage Trust for their support in enabling me to fund the digitalising of the Bulford Kiwi on Beacon Hill. The Kippenberger Literary Fund generously granted me sufficient funds to assist in the publication of the book and a small grant was received from my local Manurewa Cosmopolitan Club to help with my regular airfares to Wellington.

Like many other New Zealand families, my family has deep roots in the military history of our country, the first recorded affiliation being that of a newly arrived settler to New Zealand, Richard Jarrett from Holkham in Norfolk, joining the militia in Christchurch in the 1860s. My maternal grandfather lied about his age and travelled to South Africa to take part in the Boer War, only to find that it was all over by the time his ship arrived. My great uncles on all sides of the family fought in WWI; a number of them lie in graves dotted across all areas where New Zealanders took part in campaigns. My father and uncles, again on both sides of my family, fought in WWII, often with brothers fighting in the same battles. My husband Barry's forebears similarly took part in both wars, one returning to New Zealand after over four years' service away in WWI in time to celebrate his twenty-first birthday.

Those men's stories have been passed down through our family, and are now being told to the next generation. This is done not to glorify war but to hold their memories close and to celebrate the people they were, who we are and above all to remind us, 'Lest we forget'.

Endnotes

The Bulford Kiwi

1 *The Bulford Guide: an information handbook and directory*, p 58

PART ONE

Chapter One

1 Turnbull Library — Stokes Bertram Oliver. 1896–1994. Papers relating to service in World War One.

2 Boyack, N, and J Tolerton (1990). *In the Shadow of War* Auckland, Penguin p 242'. In an interview with Jane Tolerton and Nicolas Boyack, Bert Stokes refers to his having left Britain in March 1919 to return to New Zealand. His military record states that he left Britain in May 1919 on the *Northumberland* and arrived in NZ on 7 June 1919.

3 Jenkins, G. Collection of letters to his father 1917–1919. Used with permission from the Jenkins family.

4 Lloyd, T. Letter to his parents 1918. Used with permission from Trevor Lloyd, Wellington.

5 Turnbull Library — MS-Group 1815 Interview — Bert Stokes. World War I Oral History Archive. Ref: OHC-002770.

6 Stokes, Bertram Oliver 1896–1994. Papers relating to service in World War One. Turnbull Library.

7 Correspondence with Brigadier-General G S Richardson 1918–1919. National Archives, Allen1 1 Ministerial Files.

8 Stewart, H (1921). *The New Zealand division, 1916–1919: a popular history based on official records*. Auckland: Whitcombe and Tombs, p 605.

9 Ibid.

10 Ferguson, D (1921). *The History of the Canterbury Regiment 1914–1919* Auckland, Whitcombe and Tombs Ltd, p 287.

11 Byrne, A E (1921). *Official History of the Otago Regiment N.Z.E.F in the Great War 1914–1918* Dunedin: J Wilkie and Co Ltd, pp 384–385.

12 O'Connell, John Joseph, 1918. O'Connell, John Joseph, b 1896: Diary. Ref: MSX–8243. Alexander Turnbull Library, Wellington, New Zealand. http://natlib.govt.nz/records/22689236

13 Ibid. Note: O'Connell uses the word 'sox' in his diary which was unusual for those times. The fact that O'Connell uses it may be because prior to enlisting in the army he was a window dresser in a menswear store in Ponsonby, Auckland. The word 'sox' was used commercially in the early 1900s.

14 Ibid.

15 Ibid.

16 Crawford, J (2008). *The Devil's Own War: The First World War Diary of Brigadier-General Herbert Hart* Auckland: Exisle Publishing Ltd, p 272.

17 O'Connell, op.cit.

18 Ingram, N M (2006). *In Flanders Fields: The World War One diary of Private Monty Ingram*. Auckland: David Ling, p 162.

19 National Archives WA 133 ZG71/4 Demobilisation — General file. Demobilisation of the NZEF p 4.

Chapter Two

1 'Demobilisation Begun'. *Evening Post,* 25 November 1918. *Vol. XCV1, Issue 127,* p 5. Papers Past. Alexander Turnbull Library.

2 'On the declaration of the Armistice in November 1918, the following New Zealand troops were overseas. In France 24,115, in England 23,467 and in Egypt 4,541.' *New Zealand Official Year-book* 1919, p 255.

3 National Archives WA 133 ZG71/4 Demobilisation — General file, 5 September 1918–3 October 1919. Memo from HQ 3rd (Reserve) Battalion, Auckland Regiment to HQ 4th N.Z. Infantry (Reserve) Brigadier.

4 Young, R Brigadier-General. Collection of letters 1918. Permission to use the Young Collection has been granted by the descendants of the Young family.

5 Ibid.

6 National Library — ms-papers–7567- 1.

7 National Archives WA 133 (178) ZG 71/2/2. Demobilisation – Transfer of officers to Sling Camp for evacuation to New Zealand, 12 December 1918–14 May 1919. Note: Routine Order 57 was discovered as scrap paper to which material relating to the file was glued.

8 Rothstein, A (1980). *The Soldiers' Strikes of 1919.* London: Palgrave MacMillan UK.

9 Drew, H T B (ed.) (1923). *The War Effort of New Zealand.* Wellington: Whitcoumbe & Tombs, pp. 221–229.

Chapter Three

1 Ingram, N M (2006). *In Flanders Fields: The World War One Diary of Private Monty Ingram,* Auckland: David Ling Ltd, p 42.

2 Crawford, T S (1999).*Wiltshire and the Great War. Training the Empire's Soldiers.* Reading, DPF Publishing, p 137.

3 Dewar, D. Letter, from copies of letters held by descendants of the Dewar Family. Originals in the Hocken Library, Dunedin, MS–1510/002.

4 Ibid.

5 Ibid.

6 Boyack, N, and J Tolerton (1990). *In the Shadow of War* Auckland: Penguin, p 136.

7 Jenkins, G. Collection of letters to his father 1917–1919; Used with permission from the Jenkins family.

8 Ibid.

9 Commonwealth War Graves Commission, Tidworth Military Cemetery.

10 Sling Camp appears to have been designed to hold approxiamtely 4000 men. With 6000 housed on the camp site, the soldiers would have experienced serious overcrowding.

11 Drew, H T B (ed.) (1923) *The War Effort of New Zealand.* Wellington: Whitcombe and Tombs Ltd, p 251.

12 'The New Zealanders: Army at home' by H . B Drew, 2nd Lieut, *Ashburton Guardian,* 14 November 1918, p 2. Papers Past. Alexander Turnbull Library.

13 National Archives WA 133 (178) ZG 71/2/2 Demobilisation — Transfer of officers to Sling Camp for evacuation to New Zealand, 12 December 1918–14 May 1919. Note: Routine Order 50, 27 February 1919 was discovered as scrap paper to which material relating to the file was glued.

14 McLaren, George, 1887–1962 : World War One letters and diaries. Ref: MSX-5131. Alexander Turnbull Library, Wellington, New Zealand. http://natlib.govt.nz/records/22678816

15 National Archives ACID 15/ 6/10 Camps — Larkhill, 21 February – 28 June 1918.

16 The 21 February memo also gave clear instructions as to how the camp was to operate in order to beat the measles epidemic spreading from Sling Camp where eighteen deaths had been recorded in the first 14 days of February 1918. Larkhill was used as an isolation camp for at least a six-week period, housing men who had arrived as part of

the 35th Reinforcements and who had left New Zealand early in March 1918. The worst of the epidemic appeared to have been in Sling Camp but the precautions taken would have avoided the further spread of the disease. N A ACID 15/ 6/10 Camps — Larkhill, 21 February — 28 June 1918.

17 Townsend, Francis Payne, b 1895 : War diaries.Ref:MSX-7144.AlexanderTurnbull Library, Wellington, New Zealand. http://natlib.govt.nz/records/23171813

18 Ibid.

19 Ibid.

20 Ibid.

21 Ibid.

22 Ibid.

23 Ibid.

24 Stokes Bertram Oliver 1896–1994. Papers relating to service in World War One. Ref: MS–1815 Turnbull Library.

25 Ibid.

26 Townsend, Francis Payne, b 1895. War diaries. op.cit.

27 Ibid.

28 Ibid.

29 National Archives WA 133 ZG 28/64 Disturbance at Sling Camp [Sling riots]. Minutes from a meeting of delegates from Sling Camp held at NZEF Headquarters.

30 Townsend op.cit.

31 Raymond, I W (1924). New Zealanders in Mufti, London: Argus Printing Co. Retrieved from digital.slv.vic.gov.au/dtl_publish/pdf/marc/40/997024.html

32 Summers. J A, G D Shanks, M G Baker, and N Wilson. Severe impact of the 1918–19 pandemic influenza in a national military force. NZ Medical Journal 2103 July 12 126 (1378): pp 36–47.

Chapter Four

1 McLaren, George, 1887–1962: World War One letters and diaries. Ref: MSX-5131. Alexander Turnbull Library, Wellington, New Zealand. http://natlib.govt.nz/records/22678816

2 Cotton, B. (1988, June 18). The Day the Kiwis rioted at Sling. The Auckland Star, p 5.

3 National Archives WA 133 ZG28/64 Disturbance at Sling Camp [Sling riots]. Report by G.O i/c Administration N.Z. Troops, United Kingdom London 29-3-19

4 Townsend, Francis Payne, b 1895: War diaries.Ref:MSX-7144.AlexanderTurnbull Library, Wellington, New Zealand. http://natlib.govt.nz/records/23171813.

5 Boyack N, and Tolerton, J. (1990). In the Shadow of War. Auckland, Penguin. p242

6 Ibid.

7 Boyack, N, and Tolerton, J. (1990). op.cit. pp162-163

8 Graubard, S R. Military Demobilisation in Great Britain Following the First World War, The Journal of Modern History, 19:4 (1947) p 297.

9 'Unrest in Great Britain' (31 January 1919).Otago Daily Times Issue 17537, p 6. Papers Past. Alexander Turnbull Library.

10 Crawford, J (2008). The Devil's Own War. The First World War Diary of Brigadier-General Herbert Hart Auckland, Exisle Publishing Ltd, p 281.

11 Delayed by Strikes (8 April 1919). New Zealand Herald Vol LV1, Issue 17130, p 9. Papers Past. Alexander Turnbull Library.

12 Ibid.

13 National Archives WA133 ZG 28/64 Disturbance at Sling Camp [Sling riots]. Minutes from a meeting of delegates from Sling Camp, 15 March 1919, 24/182 Sgt A Hunter, 21858 L/C E P Miller, 2/290 Gnr P G Busing, 6/866 Pte M S Hamber, 20142 Sgt G F Hoggard, 13698 Sgt A K Christie, 8/1111 Sgt E S Skipworth, 9/1399 Cpl M Salter, 16223 Pte L Leeder, 4/1076 Sgt A R Alexander, 10005 Cpl T V Foster, 26021 Spr F A Bailey.

14 In fact six ships, which must have been on stand-by, left England bound for New Zealand between 27 March and 5 April 1919, carrying 4774 troops

between them. N A AAYS 953/49/70/188 Medical — Returning drafts to New Zealand *Remuera* (ship).

15 National Archives WA133 ZG 28/64 Disturbance at Sling Camp [Sling riots]. Minutes from a meeting of delegates from Sling Camp.

16 Wynd, M (2006). '*So the end has come … I shall see you all again*': Demobilising the New Zealand Expeditionary Force, November 1918–September 1919 (Unpublished master's thesis). Massey University, Albany, New Zealand, pp 178–179

17 N A AAYS 953/49/70/188 Medical — Returning drafts to New Zealand *Remuera* (ship). Passenger List on Voyage of R.M.S *Remuera*, Plymouth to New Zealand.

Note: An observation made by Lieutenant-Colonel J Hargest, the officer in charge of the returning troops on the *Remuera* supports many of the predictions of NZEF senior officers in late 1918 about the repatriation arrangements for the troops. Hargest said the men did not respond to their officers as he would have expected them to; they were dislocated from other men on the ship, as they had not served with them, and were strangers to the officers in charge of them.

18 Picquet is a variation of the word 'picket'. In a military context it is used to describe a soldier or small group of soldiers performing a particular duty, especially one sent out to watch for the enemy.

19 National Archives WA 133 ZG 28/64 Disturbance at Sling Camp [Sling riots]. Group Routine Order 66, 18 March 1919.

20 The Sling Dozen's enlistment dates were from 1914 to 1916.

21 National Archives AAYS 953/49/70/191 Medical — Returning drafts to New Zealand *Kia Ora* (ship).

22 The *Kia Ora* sailing on 27 March was unusually light on the ratio of officers to men. It was surprising that only fifteen officers were on board, and only five to oversee some 800 men. Officials stated that there was only room for fourteen officers. Given that the majority of men on board the ship had been involved in the Sling Camp riot and were perceived to be very hard to handle in terms of discipline, it could have been a very challenging trip. In order to avoid any possible conflict, education classes were made voluntary which appeared to help. On board were 101 sergeants many of whom who had poor interaction with the officers on board, refusing to assist in any way. It was noted by H C Nutsford, Director of Movements and Major quartering that the men had very little money and what payments were made on board were insufficient for their needs. N A AAYS 953/49/70/191 Medical – Returning drafts to New Zealand *Kia Ora* (ship).

Chapter Five

1 Stewart, A E, Brigadier-General, from a collection of Stewart papers archived by the late Bessie R Allison nee Stewart. Letter dated 22 March 1919, used with permission from the family.

2 National Archives WA133 ZG 28/64 Disturbance at Sling Camp [Sling riots], 14 March – 12 October 1919, Proceedings of Court of Enquiry/ Bulford Disturbances 11 and 12 November 1918.

3 National Archives WA133 ZG 10/19 Muster Parade Sling Camp, 18 September 1917–14 March 1919. Memo Headquarters "A" Group N.Z.E.F. Sling Camp, 14 March 1919.

4 National Archives WA1 19 10/65 Health Welfare etc. Courts of Inquiry into Riots — Sling and Bulford Camps England, 15 March–7 July 1919

5 Ibid.

6 Ibid.

7 Ibid.

8 Ibid.

9 Ibid.

10 Stewart, A E, Brigadier-General, from a collection of Stewart papers archived by the late Bessie R Allison nee Stewart. Letter dated 22 March 1919, used with permission from the family.

11 Ibid.

12 National Archives WA1 19 10/65 Health Welfare etc. Courts of Inquiry into Riots — Sling and Bulford Camps England 15 March–7 July 1919.

Chapter Six

1 Stewart, A E, Brigadier-General, from a collection of Stewart papers archived by the late Bessie R Allison nee Stewart. Letter dated 22 March 1919, used with permission from the family.

2 The Croix de Guerre is a military decoration from the Kingdom of Belgium. The medal was awarded for bravery or other military virtue to an individual.

3 National Archives WA 133 ZG 28/64. Disturbance at Sling Camp [Sling riots] 14 March–12 October 1919. Canterbury Provincial Detachment Nominal Roll of Other Ranks embarking per S.S. *Kia Ora* 1/3/19. Verso of other files.

4 National Archives WA1 19 C946 198 Health, Welfare etc. Courts of inquiry into riots — Sling and Bulford Camps, England 15 March–7 July 1919 Translation of coded cablegram 4 April 1919.

5 National Archives WA133ZG28/64. Disturbance at Sling Camp [Sling riots]. Report by G.O i/c Administration N. Z. Troops, United Kingdom London 29-3-19.

6 National Archives WA1 19 C946 198 Health, Welfare etc. Courts of inquiry into riots — Sling and Bulford Camps, England 15 March–7 July 1919. Copy of Cable Received 30/4/19 from Sir James Allen.

7 National Archives WA1 19 10/65 Health Welfare etc. Courts of Inquiry into Riots — Sling and Bulford Camps England 15 March–7 July 1919 Letter from Brigadier Young to NZEF HQ London

8 National Archives WA1 19 10/65 Health Welfare etc- Courts of Inquiry into Riots — Sling and Bulford Camps England 15 March– 7 July 1919 Letter from Colonel Hutchen.

9 National Archives WA1 19 10/65 Health Welfare etc- Courts of Inquiry into Riots — Sling and Bulford Camps England 15 March–7 July 1919 Report from NZEF HQ London to HQ Military Forces Wellington New Zealand

10 Clark, H Captain, personal diary from the Clark Collection held by descendants of the Clark family. Used with permission from the family.

11 The Sling Camp Riot (14 May 1919). *Ohinemuri Gazette Vol XXX Issue 4067*, p 3. Papers Past. Alexander Turnbull Library.

12 Stewart, A E, Brigadier-General, from a collection of Stewart papers archived by the late Bessie R Allison nee Stewart. Letter dated 22 March 1919, used with permission from the family.

13 Ibid.

Chapter Seven

1 Clark, H Captain, personal diary from the Clark Collection held by descendants of the Clark family. Used with permission from the family.

2 National Archives ZG 42/156. Emblem of New Zealand at Sling Camp, 5 February–6 September 1919.

3 Ibid.

4 There were other military contenders for the idea to carve the Kiwi figure into Beacon Hill. The memo from Brigadier-General Stewart is the only official document from a senior officer existing that states that the idea had some form of official sanction either prior to or after the riot. References to a Captain/Major L W Metcalfe and a Major/Lieutenant-Colonel A G McKenzie have been mentioned in various texts as playing a significant role in the post-riot plans to construct the Kiwi. However

when both men's service records were examined they had both left Britain on the ship *Zelandia* on 28 February 1919, so were not in the camp when the riots occurred or its aftermath but en route to New Zealand. Kate Bergamar states in Discovering Hill Figures (2008, p 65) that the idea was Colonel Meads but again there is no archival evidence that points to that being the case. After Stewart left Sling Camp Colonel Mead may have advocated for the Kiwi to be left as a legacy, taking up Stewart's idea, and he may have been involved in its construction. Certainly a senior officer would have taken a role in overseeing the project, but whether that person was Colonel Meads is unclear.

5   All army ranks awarded after 1st January 1919 were considered 'temporary ranks'. So the military records of all three men will record a lower rank at the time they were demobilised. Harry Clark had completed training for his rank as captain but was not paid for that rank. He wrote about his annoyance not being recompensed appropriately in his diary.

6   In most records about this event from that period, the British Natural History Museum is referred to as the British Museum. Email correspondence by the author with James Hamill, Curator Collections and Research Enquiries on 29 October 2015 reveals, 'In 1883, the Natural History department and collections moved from the British Museum to the newly built Natural History Museum in Kensington. Although seemingly referred to as part of the British Museum, it was run as a separate institution; and because the name "British Museum Natural History" persisted through to 1963, this has constantly caused confusion with people thinking that there are natural history collections housed at the British Museum.

7   Ng, J. 'Lo Keong, Matilda', first published in the *Dictionary of New Zealand Biography*, vol. 2, 1993. Retrieved from Te Ara — the Encyclopaedia of New Zealand, https://teara.govt.nz/en/biographies/2l15/lo-keong-matilda (accessed 29 August 2017).

8   'On Beacon Hill: New Zealand Emblem at Sling' (26 September 1919). *Marlborough Express* vol. 111, issue 228, p 3. Papers Past. Alexander Turnbull Library.

9   Looking for the Action. (1992, April). *RSA Review, 67 (2)* 14.

10 Clark, H Captain, personal diary from the Clark Collection held by descendants of the Clark family. Used with permission from the family.

11 National Army Museum, NZ, 1990:1237. Letters, Harry Clark — Sling Camp WWI.

12 'On Beacon Hill: New Zealand Emblem at Sling' (26 September 1919). *Marlborough Express* vol. 111, issue 228, p 3. Papers Past. Alexander Turnbull Library.

13 National Archives. NA WA 133 ZG 42/156. Emblem of New Zealand at Sling Camp 5 February–6 September 1919. Memo from Captain Harry Clark to Sling Camp HQ dated 12 June 1919.

14 'On Beacon Hill: New Zealand Emblem at Sling' (26 September 1919). *Marlborough Express* vol. 111, issue 228, p 3. Papers Past. Alexander Turnbull Library.

15 'On Beacon Hill: New Zealand Emblem at Sling' (26 September 1919). *Marlborough Express* vol. 111, issue 228, p 3. Papers Past. Alexander Turnbull Library.

16 Ibid.

17 National Archives. NA WA 133 ZG 42/156. Emblem of New Zealand at Sling Camp 5 February–6 September 1919. Letter of 23 August 1919, from James Ramsay, managing director Kiwi Polish Co to Captain Harry Clark at Sling Camp.

18 National Archives. NA WA 133 ZG 42/156. Emblem of New Zealand at Sling Camp 5 February–6 September 1919. Letter of 6 September 1919 from Lieutenant-Colonel commanding 'A' Group Sling

Camp to Headquarters Southern Command Salisbury.

19 National Archives. Emblem of New Zealand at Sling Camp 5 February–6 September 1919 Letter of 17 September 1919 from Lieutenant-Colonel Lawrence for the chief engineer Southern Command to 'A' Group NZEF Sling Camp.

20 National Archives. Emblem of New Zealand at Sling Camp 5 February–6 September 1919. Letter of 23 September 1919 from James Ramsay managing director of Kiwi Polish Co to Major Murton at Sling Camp.

21 Clark, H, Captain, personal diary in the Clark Collection held by descendants of the Clark family. Used with permission from the family.

22 Ibid.

PART TWO

Chapter Eight

1 'Sling Camp Veteran Visits Old Haunts' (1950, December). R.S.A. Review, 27 (2) 3.

2 National Archives AD1 1532- Memorials — Kiwi emblems sling camp 1923-1960. Letter from Brigadier –General Richardson to Colonel C Deedes, 16th January 1923.

3 Sling Camp Veteran Visits Old Haunts (1950, December). R.S.A. Review, 27 (2) 3.

4 'War memories: Salisbury Plain'. High Commissioner's Visit. (27 December 1938). Evening Post vol. CXXVI p 13. Papers Past. Alexander Turnbull Library.

5 First Bulford Kiwi Scout Group information leaflet, personal communication with John Wyeth, Codford, UK.

6 Kiwi Memorial Restoration at Bulford. (29 August 1945). Evening Post Vol CXL Issue 52-1, p 7. Papers Past. Alexander Turnbull Library.

7 'Kiwi Memorial: Recent restoration' (30 August 1945). New Zealand Herald vol. 82, issue 25294, p 4. Papers Past. Alexander Turnbull Library.

8 Cox, T, Devonshire Regiment Association secretary. Personal Communication

9 Hemi, R (2016). Bulford Kiwi digital scan. Professional Practice Fellow and lecturer at the University of Otago, School of Surveying.

Currently, the Kiwi cannot be seen from the original 1919 vantage point due to the growth of the trees at the base of Beacon Hill. Recognising this, in 2016, the author commissioned a digital scan survey to assess what differences, if any, existed between the current emblem, and the original Kiwi outline that was cut in 1919. Richard Hemi states the following; 'The surveying set out point in the old Parade Ground and used by the surveyor Victor Low was established using the original Ordinance Survey plan of Sling Camp and overlaying this with current aerial imagery. There is good agreement between features that still exist i.e. the road intersection at YMCA corner, and other old roads around the perimeter. From this overlay (and also from the long section drawing and Modern Street plan) the Parade Ground set out point was able to be located. This is estimated to be at the rear of an existing property on Auckland Rd, near the corner of Auckland and Gaza Roads.

From this 1919 set outpoint a line was determined to Stephens Mound (Beacon Hill) on the promontory behind the current Kiwi and adjacent to the eastern boundary of Sling Camp. The bearing of this line was inserted into the topographical plan of the current Kiwi outline as surveyed by Peter James-Stephen of Building Design Surveys Ltd in October 2016 in terms of OS coordinates.

To create the earlier WWI Kiwi outline over the existing image, the centroid grid reference point 6/6 needs to be positioned so that the corresponding grid layout from the scaled Blenkarne-Low drawing i.e. a horizontal to vertical ratio of 1: 4.5 could be used. It was assumed that the hill sloped at approximately 10 degrees and this agrees with the 2016 topographical plan using an average slope from top to bottom of current Kiwi. Further, when the angle of elevation of approximately 4 degrees from the Parade Ground up to the centroid reference point on the hillside (an increase of height of roughly 50m) is added to the distortion required from viewers' perspective - then the ratio applied by the original survey layout is generally correct.

However the position of 6/6 can only be estimated in relation to the position of the current Kiwi and the line of bearing to Stephens Mound. It was anticipated that when the Kiwi was re-dug in 1948 a long and relatively straight line of turf along the Kiwi's back may have been recognisable. The Kiwi eye and line of the back were ultimately used to estimate the position of the centroid point. Once the centroid point was located the remaining grid lines – 2 to 11 top to bottom, and 1 to 13 across - were laid out in plan allowing the intersection points of the Kiwi design outline between these grids to be scaled and plotted, from the Blenkarne-Low drawing.'

10 First Bulford Kiwi Scout Group information leaflet, personal communication with John Wyeth, Codford UK.

11 Ibid.

Chapter Nine

1 National Archives AD1 1532. Memorials — Kiwi emblems sling camp 1923–1960. Letter from The Kiwi Polish Co Ltd to the army secretary, 26 February 1951

2 National Archives AD1 1532. Memorials — Kiwi emblems sling camp 1923–1960. Letter from the London High Commissioner W J Jordan to the Minister of Defence, 6 July 1950

3 National Archives AD1 1532. Memorials — Kiwi emblems sling camp 1923–1960. Letter from The Kiwi Polish Co to Percy Blenkarne, 23 June 1950.

4 National Archives AD1 1532. Memorials — Kiwi emblems sling camp 1923–1960. Letter from the London High Commissioner W J Jordan to the Minister of Defence, 6 July 1950

5 Ibid.

6 National Archives AD1 1532. Memorials — Kiwi emblems sling camp 1923–1960. Note by Minister of Defence attached to the official Kiwi Polish Co postcard of the Bulford Kiwi.

7 National Archives AD1 1532. Memorials — Kiwi emblems sling camp 1923–1960. Letter from Minister of Defence to the General Secretary of NZRSA, 10 November 1050

8 Ibid.

9 National Archives AAFD W2347 811 Box 78 CAB 263/3/5. Memorials Emblem at Sling Camp 1950. Memorandum for Cabinet.

10 Ibid.

11 National Archives AAFD W2347 811 Box 78 CAB 263/3/5. Memorials Emblem at Sling Camp 1950- Memorandum for the Minister of Defence, 25 October 1950.

12 Ibid.

13 'Sling Camp Emblem: R.S.A. Wants It Preserved' (1950, November). *R.S.A. Review*, 27(1), 9.

14 Ibid.

15 National Archives AD1 1532. Memorials — Kiwi emblems sling camp 1923–1960. Letters from T M Ramsay Managing Director The Kiwi Polish Co to the Editor of the RSA Review and the Minister of Defence, 9 November 1950.

16 Ibid.

17 Ibid.

18 National Archives AD1 1532. Memorials — Kiwi emblems sling camp 1923–1960. Letter from The Kiwi Polish Co to Percy Blenkarne, 23 June 1950.

19 National Archives AD1 1532. Memorials

— Kiwi emblems sling camp 1923–1960. Draft of letter from the Minister of Defence to T M Ramsay Kiwi Polish Co Ltd, 23 November 1950.

20 National Archives AD1 1532. Memorials — Kiwi emblems sling camp 1923–1960. Letter from the Army secretary to T M Ramsay Kiwi Polish Co Ltd, 1 December 1950.

21 'The Sling Camp Kiwi'. (1951, January). *R.S.A. Review,* 27 (3), 9

22 National Archives AD1 1532. Memorials — Kiwi emblems sling camp 1923–1960. Letter from T M Ramsay to the Army Secretary, 26 February 1951.

23 National Archives AD1 1532- Memorials — Kiwi emblems sling camp 1923–1960. Memo from the Army Secretary to the Minister of Defence, 13 March 1951.

24 National Archives AD1 1532. Memorials — Kiwi emblems sling camp 1923–1960. Copy of letter sent to T M Ramsay from the Minister of Defence, 12 April 1951.

25 National Archives AD1 1532. Memorials — Kiwi emblems sling camp 1923–1960. Letter sent by W J Jordan to the Minister of Defence, July 1951.

26 National Archives AD1 1532. Memorials — Kiwi emblems sling camp 1923–1960. Letter sent from Mr Bonner to Mr Percy Blenkarne.

27 National Archives AD1 1532. Memorials — Kiwi emblems sling camp 1923–1960. Report from unknown author regarding the state of the Bulford Kiwi, dated 7 December 1953.

28 National Archives AD1 1532. Memorials — Kiwi emblems sling camp 1923–1960. Report from Brigadier M B C Senior Army Liaison Officer, dated 2nd April 1954.

29 National Archives AD1 1532. Memorials — Kiwi emblems sling camp 1923–1960. Army minute 276/3/17. Subject, Maintenance Kiwi Emblem.

30 OIA to author, 25 July 2016.

31 Ibid.

Chapter Ten

1 Mackness, D, Lieutenant Colonel (2016, November 24). Personal Communication. Note: After WWI officer's ranks were changed. There were no hyphens between categories of ranks.

2 James, N D G (1987). *Plain Soldiering: A History of the armed Forces on Salisbury Plain.* Salisbury, England: The Hobnob Press p 113.

3 Kiwi to get a Shine. (1980 August). *R.S.A. Review,* 58 (4) 3.

4 Ibid.

5 New Zealand Parliament. Order papers of the House of Representatives of New Zealand [1980]. Order Paper 64(1405).

6 Riddell, O (1980, September 17). 'A war memorial the Govt has turned its back on', *The Press,* p 2.

7 Ibid.

8 Ibid.

9 Moore, M, Right Hon. (2017, May 16). Interview.

10 Ace Mobile Force Europe (Land)

11 Fisher, D, Lieutenant Colonel (2016, November 15). Interview.

12 Ibid.

13 Bartlett, D, S Bushby, and M Fitzpatrick (2016, November 25). Personal Communication.

14 Fielding, S (2016, December 7). Personal Communication.

15 Fisher, D Lieutenant Colonel (2017, January 26). Personal Communication, referenced
Admiral Grace Murray Hopper, an American Navy Rear Admiral 1906–1992.

16 Ibid.

17 Cook, J, Brigadier (2017, March 4). Personal Communication.

18 Oldfield, P, Colonel (2016 November 21). Interview.

19 Lawton, S, Colonel. (2016, November 24). Personal Communication.

20 Mackness, D, Lieutenant Colonel. (2016, November 24). Personal Communication

21 Fisher, D, Lieutenant Colonel (2017, November 15). Interview.

Postscript

1   Heritage England (2017). *Kiwi Chalk Figure above Bulford Camp*. Retrieved from https://historicengland.org.uk/listing/the-list/list-entry/1443438

2   On Beacon Hill: New Zealand Emblem at Sling. (26 September 1919). *Marlborough Express* vol. 111, issue 228, p 3. Papers Past. Alexander Turnbull Library.

Bibliography

Aitken, A (1963). *Gallipoli to the Somme: Recollections of a New Zealand Infantryman.* London: Oxford University Press.

Baker, P (1988). *King and Country Call.* Auckland, Auckland University Press.

Barton, P (2010). *Arras: the spring 1917 offensive in panoramas including Vimy Ridge and Bullecourt.* London: Constable.

Bergamar, K (2008). *Discovering Hill Figures: White Horses and other creatures of the downs, their history, location and legends.* Oxford: Shire Publications.

Best, N (2008). *The Greatest Day in History: How the Great War Really Ended.* London: Weidenfeld and Nicholson.

Blythe, R (2010). *The Age of Illusion: England in the Twenties and Thirties 1919–1940.* London: Faber Finds.

Boyack, N (1989). *Behind the Lines: The Lives of New Zealand Soldiers in the First World War.* Wellington, Allen and Unwin.

Boyack, N and J. Tolerton (eds) (1990). *In the Shadow of War: New Zealand Soldiers Talk About World War One and Their Lives.* Auckland, Penguin Books.

Brereton, C B, and J H Gray (eds) (2015). *Tales of Three Campaigns: a soldier's plain unvarnished story of a part played by New Zealanders in the Great War.* Christchurch, New Zealand: John Douglas Publishing.

Bridger, G. (2013). *The Great War Handbook.* Barnsley, United Kingdom: Pen and Sword Books.

Bulford Guide, The (nd). An information handbook and directory.

Byrne, A E (1921). *Official History of the Otago Regiment N.Z.E.F in the Great War 1914–1918.* Dunedin: J Wilkie and Co Ltd.

Burton, O E (1922). *The Auckland Regiment*. Auckland: Whitcombe and Tombs.

Burton, O E (1935). *The Silent Division: New Zealanders at the Front*. Sydney: Angus and Robertson.

Churchill. W S Right Hon. (1941, 1944 printing). *The Aftermath: being a sequel to The World Crisis*. London: Macmillan.

Churchill. W S Right Hon. (2007). *The World Crisis, 1911–1918: with an introduction by Martin Gilbert*. London: Penguin Classics.

Cotton, B (1988, June 18). The Day the Kiwis rioted at Sling. *Auckland Star*, p.5.

Cowan, J (2004). *The Maoris in the Great War: a history of the New Zealand Native Contingent and Pioneer Battalion, Gallipoli, 1915, France and Flanders 1916–1918*. Uckfield, England: Naval & Military Press.

Crawford, J (ed.) (2008). *The Devil's Own War: the First World War diary of Brigadier-General Herbert Hart*. Auckland, New Zealand: Exisle Publishing Ltd.

Crawford, J., and I McGibbon (eds) (2003). *One Flag, One Queen, One Tongue: New Zealand, the British Empire and the South African War, 1899–1902*. Auckland: Auckland University Press.

Crawford, J, and I McGibbon (eds) (2007). *New Zealand's Great War: New Zealand, the Allies and the First World War*. Auckland, New Zealand: Exisle Publishing Ltd. Crawford, T S (1999). *Wiltshire and the Great War: Training the Empire's Soldiers*. Reading, DPF Publishing.

Cunningham, W H, C A L Treadwell, and J S Hanna (1928). *The Wellington Regiment N.Z.E.F., 1914–1919*. Wellington, Ferguson and Osborn.

Department of National Defence, Canada (1962). *Canadian Expeditionary Force*. Canada: Canadian Army.

Drew, H T B (ed.) (1923). *The War Effort of New Zealand*. Wellington: Whitcombe and Tombs.

Fenton, D (2013). *New Zealand and the First World War 1914-1918*. Auckland: Penguin.

Ferguson, D (1921). *The History of the Canterbury Regiment 1914–1919*. Auckland: Whitcombe and Tombs.

Fussell, P (2009). *The Great War and Modern Memory*. New York: Sterling.

Godley, General Sir Alexander. (1939). *Life of an Irish Soldier: Reminiscences of General Sir Alexander Godley*. London: John Murray.

Graubard, S R 'Military Demobilisation in Great Britain Following the First World War', *The Journal of Modern History*, 19:4 (1947), pp 297–311

Graves, R, and A Hodge (1985). *The Long Weekend: A social history of Great Britain 1918–1939*. London: Hutchinson.

Gregory, A. (1994). *The Silence of Memory: Armistice Day 1919–1946*. Oxford: Berg Publishers.

Heritage England (2017). *Kiwi Chalk Figure above Bulford Camp*. Retrieved from https://historicengland.org.uk/listing/the-list/list-entry/1443438

Ingram, N M (2006). *In Flanders Fields: The World War One diary of private Monty Ingram*. Auckland, New Zealand: David Ling.

James, N.D.G. (1987). *Plain Soldiering: A history of the armed forces on Salisbury Plain*. Salisbury, England: The Hobnob Press.

Latter, E (1992). *Marching Onward. The History of the 2nd Battalion (Canterbury, Nelson, Marlborough, West Coast) Royal New Zealand Infantry Regiment*. Christchurch: The 2nd Battalion (Canterbury, Nelson, Marlborough, West Coast) Royal New Zealand Infantry Regiment.

Lloyd, N (2013). *Hundred Days: the end of the Great War*. London: Viking Press.

McDonald, W [compiler] (2013). *Honours and Awards to the New Zealand Expeditionary Force in the Great War 1914–1918*. Hamilton: Richard Stowers.

McGibbon, I (1991). *The Path to Gallipoli: Defending New Zealand 1840–1915*. Wellington: GP Books.

McGibbon, I (2002). *Kiwi Sapper: the Corps of Royal New Zealand Engineers' Century of Service*. Auckland, New Zealand: Reed.

McGibbon, I (2000). *The Oxford Companion to New Zealand Military History*. Oxford: Oxford University Press.

Marwick, A (2006) *The Deluge: British Society and the First World War*. London: Palgrave.

Millen, J (1997). *Salute to Service: a history of the Royal New Zealand Corps of Transport and its predecessors, 1860–1996*. Wellington: Victoria University Press.

Mulligan, W (2014). *The Great War for Peace*. New Haven: Yale University Press.

Newman, P (1997). *The Lost Gods of Albion: The chalk hill figures of Britain*. Somerset, Great Britain: Sutton Publishing.

New Zealand Parliament [1980]. Order papers of the House of Representatives of New Zealand. Order Paper 64(1405).

New Zealand Official Year-Book 1919. Wellington, New Zealand: Government Printer.

Ng, James (1993). 'Lo Keong, Matilda', first published in the *Dictionary of New Zealand Biography*, vol. 2, 1993. Te Ara — the Encyclopaedia of New Zealand, https://teara.govt.nz/en/biographies/2l15/lo-keong-matilda (accessed 29 August 2017)

Nicholson, Colonel G W L (1962). *Canadian Expeditionary Force 1914–1919: The official history of the Canadian Army in the First World War*. Ottawa, Canadian Department of National Defence.

Nicolson, J (2009). *The Great Silence: 1918–1920: Living in the shadow of the Great War*. London: John Murray Publishers.

Perry, F W (1988). *The Commonwealth Armies: Manpower and organisation in two world wars*. Manchester: Manchester Press.

Peters, S T (2005). *The 1918 Influenza Pandemic*. New York: Benchmark Books.

Phillips, J, N Boyack, and E P Malone (eds) (1988). *The Great*

Adventure: New Zealand soldiers describe the First World War. Wellington, New Zealand: Allen and Unwin/Port Nicholson Press.

Pugsley, C (1991). *On the Fringes of Hell.* Auckland: Hodder and Stoughton.

Pugsley, C (1995). *Te Hokowhitu a Tu: the Maori Pioneer Battalion in the First World War.* Auckland: Reed.

Pugsley, C (1996). *Gallipoli: the New Zealand Story.* Auckland, New Zealand: Sceptre.

Pugsley, C (2004). *The Anzac Experience: New Zealand, Australia and Empire in the First World War.* Auckland, New Zealand: Reed.

Pugsley, C (2014). *Fighting for Empire: New Zealand and the Great War of 1914–1918.* Auckland: Bateman.

Pugsley, C, L Barber, B Mikaere, N Prickett, and R Young (1996). *Scars on the Heart: Two Centuries of New Zealand at War.* Auckland, New Zealand: Bateman in association with Auckland Museum.

Raymond, I W (1924). New *Zealanders in Mufti.* London: Argus Printing Co. Retrieved from digital.slv.vic.gov.au/dtl_publish/pdf/marc/40/997024.html

Riddell, O (1980, September 17). 'A war memorial the Govt has turned its back on'. Christchurch: *The Press,* p 25.

Rothstein, A (1980). *The Soldier's Strikes of 1919.* London: Palgrave MacMillan UK.

R.S.A. (1950, November). 'Sling Camp Emblem: R.S.A. Wants It Preserved'. *R.S.A. Review,* 27 (1), p 9.

R.S.A. (1950, December). 'Sling Camp Veteran Visits Old Haunts'. *R.S.A. Review,* 27 (2) 3.

R.S.A. (1951, January). 'The Sling Camp Kiwi'. *R.S.A. Review,* 27 (3), p 9.

R.S.A. (1980, August). 'Kiwi to get a Shine'. *R.S.A Review,* 58 (4) 3.

R.S.A. (1980, October). 'Army Volunteers Rescue Ailing Bulford Kiwi'. *R.S.A. Review,* p 1.

R.S.A. (1991, August). 'Giant Kiwi Integral Part of Bulford Camp…' *R.S.A. Review,* 67 (4) 21.

R.S.A. (1992, April). 'Looking for the Action'. *R.S.A Review,* 67(2) 14.

Seaman, L C B (1966). *Post-Victorian Britain, 1902–1951.* London: Methuen.

Seddon, T E Y (1968). *The Seddons: an autobiography.* Auckland: Collins.

Sheffield, G (1999). *Leadership in the Trenches: Officer-man relations, morale and discipline in the British army in the era of the First World War.* Basingstoke: Macmillan.

Smith, G (1980, December). 'Bird on the hill'. *Soldier Magazine,* 36 (12), pp 56–57.

Stewart, H (1921). *The New Zealand Division, 1916–1919: A popular history based on official records.* Auckland: Whitcombe and Tombs.

Strohn, M (ed.) (2013). *World War I Companion.* Oxford: Osprey Publishing.

Summers, J A, G D Shanks, M G Baker, and N Wilson (2013, July). 'Severe Impact of the 1918–19 Pandemic Influenza in a Military Force'. *The New Zealand Medical Journal,* Vol. 126, No. 1378. pp 36–47.

Taylor, W (1978). *The Twilight Hour: A personal account of World War I.* Morrinsville: Sutherland.

Thomson, J (2000). *Warrior Nation: New Zealanders at the front, 1900–2000.* Christchurch: Hazard Press.

Tolerton, J (2013). *An Awfully Big Adventure: World War One veterans tell their stories: from interviews for the World War One Oral History archive.* Auckland: Penguin.

Webb, S (2016). *1919: Britain's Year of Revolution.* Barnsley, South Yorkshire: Pen and Sword History.

Weintraub, S (1987). *A Stillness Heard Around the World: The end of the Great War, November 1918.* New York: Dutton.

Wilkie, A H (1924). *Official War History of the Wellington Mounted Rifles Regiment: 1914–1919.* Auckland: Whitcombe and Tombs.

Wolfe, R (1991). *Kiwi: More than a bird.* Auckland, New Zealand: Random Century.

Wood, F L W (1958). *New Zealand in the World*. Wellington, War History Branch, Dept of Internal Affairs.

Wood, F L W (1958). *The New Zealand People at War: Political and external affairs*. Wellington: War History Branch, Dept of Internal Affairs.

Wynd, M (2006). 'So the end has come . . . I shall see you all again: Demobilising the New Zealand Expeditionary Force, November 1918–September 1919' (Unpublished master's thesis). Albany, New Zealand: Massey University.

Alexander Turnbull Library Resources

McLaren, George, 1887–1962: World War One letters and diaries. Ref: MSX-5131. http://natlib.govt.nz/records/22678816

O'Connell, John Joseph, 1918. O'Connell, John Joseph, b 1896: Diary. Ref: MSX- 8243. http://natlib.govt.nz/records/22689236

Stokes, Bertram Oliver (1896–1994). Papers relating to service in World War One. Ref: MS-1815 Turnbull Library

Townsend, Francis Payne, b 1895: War diaries. Ref: MSX-7144. http://natlib.govt.nz/records/23171813

Demobilisation papers — ms-papers-7567-1.

Interviews:

Interview with Albert Simpson, tape three
Date: 3 Oct 1989 From: World War I Oral History Archive Ref: OHC-002754 Interviewer(s) - Jane Tolerton Interviewer(s) - Nicholas Boyack Arrangement: Tape sequence - 3 of 3 Quantity: 1 C60 cassette(s).

Interview with Bert Hughes, printed abstract
Date: 4 Nov 1989 From: World War I Oral History Archive Ref: OHA-0480 Quantity: 1 printed abstract(s).

Interview with Bert Hughes, tape three
Date: 4 Nov 1989 From: World War I Oral History Archive Ref: OHC-002658Interviewer(s) — Jane Tolerton Interviewer(s) -

Nicholas Boyack Arrangement: Tape sequence - 3 of 3 Quantity: 1 C60 cassette(s)

Interview with Bertram Stokes

Date: 13 Sept 1988 From: World War I Oral History Archive Ref: OHC-002766Interviewer(s) - Jane Tolerton

Interviewer(s) - Nicholas Boyack Arrangement: Tape sequence - 1 of 5 Quantity: 1 C60 cassette(s).

Interview with Bertram Stokes, tape four

Date: 13 Sept 1988 From: World War I Oral History Archive Ref: OHC-002769Interviewer(s) - Jane Tolerton

Interviewer(s) - Nicholas Boyack Arrangement: Tape sequence - 4 of 5 Quantity: 1 C60 cassette(s).

Interview with Bertram Stokes, tape five

Date: 13 Sept 1988 From: World War I Oral History Archive Ref: OHC-002770Interviewer(s) - Jane Tolerton

Interviewer(s) - Nicholas Boyack Arrangement: Tape sequence - 5 of 5 Quantity: 1 C60 cassette(s).

Interview with James Frederick Blakemore, digital abstract

Date: 5 Aug 1988 From: World War I Oral History Archive Ref: OHDL-000306 Quantity: 1 Electronic document(s)

Interview with John Eric Beveridge

Date: 19 Jul 1988 From: World War I Oral History Archive Ref: OHC-002554 Interviewer(s) - Jane Tolerton

Interviewer(s) - Nicholas Boyack Arrangement: Tape sequence - 3 of 3 Quantity: 1 C60 cassette(s).

Interview with Joseph Dwyer, tape two

Date: 5 Oct 1988 From: World War I Oral History Archive Ref: OHC-002615 Interviewer(s) - Jane Tolerton

Interviewer(s) - Nicholas Boyack Arrangement: Tape sequence - 2 of 2 Quantity: 1 C60 cassette(s).

Interview with Lieutenant-Colonel Lawrence Morris Blyth, tape four

Date: 28 Sept 1988 and 20 Oct 1988 From: World War I Oral History Archive Ref: OHC-002566 Interviewer(s) –

Jane Tolerton Interviewer(s) - Nicholas Boyack Arrangement: Tape
    sequence - 4 of 7 Quantity: 1 C60 cassette(s).
Interview with Lieutenant-Colonel Lawrence Morris Blyth, tape six
Date: 28 Sept 1988 and 20 Oct 1988 From: World War I Oral History
    Archive Ref: OHC-002568 Interviewer(s) -
Jane Tolerton Interviewer(s) - Nicholas Boyack Arrangement: Tape
    sequence - 6 of 7 Quantity: 1 C60 cassette(s).
Interview with William Thomas Cubbon, tape three
Date: 5 Nov 1989 From: World War I Oral History Archive Ref:
    OHC-002604Interviewer(s) - Jane Tolerton
Interviewer(s) - Nicholas Boyack Arrangement: Tape sequence - 3 of 3
    Quantity: 1 C60 cassette(s).

Papers Past, Alexander Turnbull Library
'Delayed by Strikes' (8 April 1919). *New Zealand Herald* Vol LV1,
    Issue 17130, p 9.
'Demobilisation Begun' (25 November 1918). *Evening Post,* Vol
    XCV1, Issue 127, p 5.
Drew, H T B (14 November 1918). 'The New Zealanders: Army at
    home. *Ashburton Guardian,* p 2.
'Kiwi Memorial: Recent restoration.' (30 August 1945). *New Zealand
    Herald* Vol 82, Issue 25294, p 4.
'Kiwi Memorial Restoration at Bulford' (29 August 1945). *Evening
    Post* Vol CXL Issue 52–1, p 7.
'On Beacon Hill: New Zealand Emblem at Sling' (26 September
    1919). *Marlborough* Express Vol III,
Issue 228, p 3.
'The Sling Camp Riot' (14 May 1919) *Ohinemuri Gazette* Vol XXX
    Issue 4067, p 3.
'Unrest in Great Britain'. (31 January 1919).*Otago Daily Times* Issue
    17537, p 6.
'War memories: Salisbury Plain. High Commissioner's Visit' (27
    December 1938). *Evening Post* Vol CXXVI, p 13.

Auckland Central City Library

Sir George Grey Special Collections, Auckland Libraries, NZ Print
966 (artist: Charles E H Putt)

National Archives New Zealand Wellington Office

NA AAFD W2347 811 Box 78 CAB 263/3/5 Memorials. Emblem at
Sling Camp 1950.

NA AAYS 953/49/70/188 Medical. Returning drafts to New Zealand
Remuera (ship).

NA AAYS 953/49/70/191 Medical. Returning drafts to New Zealand
Kia Ora (ship).

NA ACID 15/ 6/10 Camps. Larkhill, 21 February–28 June 1918.

NA ACID 17/ 10/24 Health, Welfare, etc. Influenza Epidemic –
General Correspondence 5 November 1918–29 May 1919.

NA AD1 1532 Memorials. Kiwi emblems sling camp 1923–1960.

NA — Allen1 1 Ministerial Files. Correspondence with Brigadier-
General GS Richardson 1918–1919.

NA WA133 ZG 10/19 Muster Parade Sling Camp, 18 September
1917–14 March 1919.

NA WA133 ZG 28/64 Disturbance at Sling Camp [Sling riots] 14
March–12 October 1919.

NA WA133 ZG71/4 Demobilisation. General file.

NA WA133 (178) ZG 71/2/2 Demobilisation. Transfer of officers to
Sling Camp for evacuation to New Zealand, 12 December 1918–
14 May 1919.

NA WA119 10/65 Health Welfare etc. Courts of Inquiry into Riots —
Sling and Bulford Camps England 15 March–7 July 1919.

NA ZG 42/156 Emblem of New Zealand at Sling Camp, 5 February–
6 September 1919.

National Archives Wellington: Army Service Records

Alexander, Alick Robert. Service Number 4/1076*

Bailey, Frederick Arthur. Service Number: 26021*

Beveridge, John Eric. Service Number: 18058.

Blakemore, James Frederick. Service Number: 14930

Blenkarne, Percy Cecil. Service Number: 78001

Blyth, Lawrence Morris. Service Number: 26/332

Busing, George Percival. Service Number: 2/290*

Clark, Henry Masterton. Service Number: 4/386

Crozier, Frederick Gwynn. Service Number: 29648**

Cubbon, William Thomas. Service Number: 25478

Christie, Andrew Kenrick. Service Number13698*

Davidson Thomas. Service Number: 75486

Dewar, David. Service Number 18211

Dwyer Joseph. Service Number: 14082

Foster, Thomas Victor. Service Number 10005*

Fuller, Edward Geoffrey. Service Number: 23820**

Griffin, Joseph Gerald. Service Number: 2/3000**

Hamber, Maurice Straight. Service Number: 6/866*

Hoggard, Gerald Francis. Service Number: 20142*

Hunter, Arthur. Service Number: 24/182*

Ingram, Neil Montague. Service Number: 42110

Jenkins, George Arthur. Service Number: 51567

Jordan, William Joseph. Service Number 54524

Lawry R.L R. Service Number: 6/1105

Leeder, Leslie. Service Number: 16223*

Lloyd, Trevor. Service Number: 62095

Low, Victor Thomas. Service Number: 37663

MacDonald, Thomas Lachlan. Service Number: 13300

McKenzie, Alexander George. Service Number: 10067

McLaren, George. Service Number: 12/2419

Mead, Owen Herbert. Service Number: 6/296

Melvill, Charles William. Service Number: 15/35

Metcalfe Louis Wilfred. Service Number: 14348
Miller, Edward Percival. Service Number: 21858*
O'Connell, John. Service Number: 58079
Putt, Charles Earnest Henry. Service Number: 54390
Richardson, Sir George Spafford. Service Number: 15/209
Rutherford, John Thomas. Service Number: 4/1995**
Salter, Martin. Service Number: 9/1399*
Skipworth, Edward Stephen. Service Number: 8/1111*
Stewart, Alexander Edward. Service Number: 24/1
Stewart, Hugh. Service Number: 6/982
Stokes, Bertram Oliver. Service Number: 25038
Townsend, Francis Payne. Service Number: 24/603
Young, Robert. Service Number: 10/451

* The Sling Dozen
** Not at the meeting with the NZEF HQ on March but part of the liaison group in Sling Camp afterwards, replacing Alexander, Hoggard, Christie and Foster. All returned to New Zealand in May 1919.
*** None of the eight men court martialled is listed.

National Army Museum

National Army Museum, NZ: 1990.1237 Letters, Harry Clark — Sling Camp WW1.
National Army Museum, NZ: 2009.97 Plan of Chalk Kiwi.jpg.
National Army Museum, NZ: 1992.2626 The Chalk Kiwi - Kiwi Polish Co

Unpublished personal papers, interviews and communication

Bartlett, D, Bushby, S, and Fitzpatrick, M, (2016, November 25). Personal Communication.
Brown, B J B (2016). Bulford Kiwi drawings.
Clark, H Captain, personal diary from the Clark Collection held by

descendants of the Clark family. Used with permission from the family.

Clark, H Captain, restored images from negatives dated 1919 in the Clark Collection held by descendants of the Clark family. Used with permission from the family.

Cook, J, Brigadier (2017, March 4). Personal Communication.

Dewar, D. Letter, from copies of letters held by descendants of the Dewar Family. Originals in the Hocken Library, Dunedin, MS-1510/002.

Fielding, S (2016, December 7). Personal Communication.

First Bulford Kiwi Scout Group information leaflet, personal communication with John Wyeth, Codford UK.

Fisher, D, Lieutenant Colonel (2016, November 15). Interview

Fisher, D, Lieutenant Colonel (2017, January 26). Personal Communication

Hemi, R (2016). Bulford Kiwi digital scan. Professional Practice Fellow and lecturer at the University of Otago, School of Surveying.

Jenkins, G. Collection of letters to his father 1917–1919. Used with permission from the Jenkins' family.

Jenkins, G. Photograph and drawings from the Jenkins Collection. Used with permission from the Jenkins' family.

Lawton, S, Colonel (2016, November 24). Personal Communication.

Lloyd, T. Letter to his parents 1918. Used with permission from Trevor Lloyd Wellington.

Mackness, D, Lieutenant Colonel (2016, November 24). Personal Communication.

Moore, M, Right Hon. (2017, May 16). Personal Interview.

Oldfield, P, Colonel (2016 November 21). Interview.

Stewart, A E, Brigadier-General, from a collection of Stewart papers archived by the late Bessie R Allison nee' Stewart. Letter dated 22 March 1919, used with permission from the family.

Stewart, A E, Brigadier-General, from a collection of Stewart papers archived by the late Bessie R Allison nee' Stewart. Photographs of

Brigadier-General Stewart addressing New Zealand troops at Sling Camp in March 1919 used with permission from the family.

Young, R, Brigadier-General. Collection of letters 1918. Used with permission from the descendants of the Young family.

Picture credits

Cover and jacket: (front) Montage of, from left, Brigadier-General Stewart [James Hardie Neil Album (1914–18). Portrait of A E Stewart. Neil, J. Auckland War Memorial Museum Tamaki Paenga Hira. PH-ALB-195-p15-lp1.]; George Jenkins [The Jenkins Collectiom, used with permission of the Jenkins Family.]; Percy Blenkarne [The Blenkarne Collection. Used with permission from the family.]; and Harry Clark [The Clark Collection. Used with permission from the family.], with the outline of the Bulford Kiwi and a map of Sling Camp [The National Archives, UK, WO 32/4055, Bulford Sling Camp 1921.]; (back) Harry Clark [The Clark Collection. Used with permission from the family.] and Victor Low [detail, from 'The Klink: Souvenir of the voyage of H.M.N.Z.T. *Turakina*, 1917'. Sue Baker Wilson Collection.]

Page 5: Bertie Jarrett with his parents. Personal Collection.

Page 10: General Brian Poananga and Lieutentant Colonel Danny Fisher, Danny Fisher Collection.

Page 38: Map an adaptation of the 'NZEF in England 1916–19 map', URL: https://nzhistory.govt.nz/media/photo/nzef-england-1916-19-map, (Ministry for Culture and Heritage), updated 8-Dec-2016.

Page 40: George Jenkins, The Jenkins Collectiom, used with permission of the Jenkins Family.

Pages 44–45: Charles E H Putt drawing. Sir George Grey Special Collections, Auckland Libraries, NZ Print 966 (artist: Charles E H Putt).

Page 46–47: The National Archives, UK, WO 32/4055, Bulford Sling Camp 1921.

Page 55: Stewart, A. E., Brigadier-General, from a collection of Stewart papers archived by the late Bessie R. Allison nee' Stewart. Photographs of Brigadier-General Stewart addressing New Zealand troops at Sling Camp in March 1919 used with permission from the family. The photograph was given to Brigadier General Stewart by a soldier J.S Reid. On the back of the photograph is written 'Father addressing rioters Sling Camp England Mar 1919.'

Page 71: Stewart, A E, Brigadier-General, from a collection of Stewart papers archived by the late Bessie R Allison nee Stewart. Photographs of Brigadier-General Stewart addressing New Zealand troops at Sling Camp in March 1919, used with permission from the family. The photograph was given to Brigadier-General Stewart by a soldier, J S Reid, who wrote on the back of it, 'taken by a "digger" I know who was on the scene at the time'.

Page 85, top: Alexander Turnbull Library, Wellington, New Zealand [C-109-020. ATL].

Page 85, bottom: Drawings reproduced by permission of the Lloyd family.

Page 88, top left: Percy Blenkarne, The Blenkarne Collection. Used with permission from the family.

Page 88, top right: Harry Clark, The Clark Collection. Used with permission from the family.

Page 88, bottom: Victor Low, 'The Klink: Souvenir of the voyage of H.M.N.Z.T. *Turakina*, 1917'. Sue Baker Wilson Collection.

Page 91, top: Kiwi from the British Natural History Museum. © Trustees of the British Natural History Museum.

Page 91, bottom: National Army Museum, NZ: 2009.97 Plan of Chalk Kiwi.jpg

Page 92: Clark, H Captain, restored images from negatives dated 1919 in the Clark Collection held by descendants of the Clark family. Used with permission from the family.

Page 93, top: Brown, B J B (2016). Bulford Kiwi drawings

Page 93, bottom: Brown, B J B (2016). Bulford Kiwi drawings

Page 94: Clark, H Captain, restored images from negatives dated 1919 in the Clark Collection held by descendants of the Clark family. Used with permission from the family.

Page 94: Brown, B J B (2016). Bulford Kiwi drawings

Page 97: Brown, B J B (2016). Bulford Kiwi drawings

Page 101: Clark, H Captain, restored images from negatives dated 1919 in the Clark Collection held by descendants of the Clark family. Used with permission from the family.

Page 102: Clark, H Captain, restored images from negatives dated 1919 in the Clark Collection held by descendants of the Clark family. Used with permission from the family.

Page 103: National Army Museum, NZ: 1992.2626 The Chalk Kiwi - Kiwi Polish Company.

Page 110: From the Jenkins Collection. Used with permission from the Jenkins family. Published in, Sling Camp Veteran Visits Old Haunts. (1950, December). R.S.A. *Review*, 27 (2) 3.

Page 111: Jenkins, G. Photograph and drawings from the Jenkins Collection. Used with permission from the Jenkins' family.

Page 113: Brown, B J B. (2016). Bulford Kiwi drawings (both images).

Page 114: Hemi, R. (2016) Bulford Kiwi digital scan. Professional Practice Fellow and lecturer at the University of Otago, School of Surveying.

Page 131: Pratt, R. photographer (1980). In Smith, G. 'Bird on the hill'. *Soldier Magazine,* 36 (12), 56–57).

Page 132: Pratt, R. photographer (1980). In Smith, G. 'Bird on the hill'. *Soldier Magazine*, 36 (12), 56–57).

Page 133: Pratt, R. photographer (1980). In Smith, G. 'Bird on the hill'. *Soldier Magazine*, 36 (12), 56–57).

Page 134: Pratt, R. photographer (1980). In Smith, G. 'Bird on the hill'. *Soldier Magazine*, 36 (12), 56–57).

Page 137: Nolan, R. Cpl RLC. (2007, July). 'Facelift for the Bulford Kiwi'. *Drumbeat*: Tidworth, Netheravon and Bulford Community Newsletter Issue 122 p 1.

Page 139: Danny Fisher, 1980. Pratt, R. photographer (1980). In Smith, G. 'Bird on the hill'. *Soldier Magazine*, 36 (12), 56–57) and Clark, H, Captain, in the Clark Collection held by descendants of the Clark family. Used with permission from the family.

index